Checklist for Life
for Moms

Presented To:

_____

Presented By:

_____

Date:

_____

Checklist for Life
for Moms

Checklist for Life
for Moms

NELSON BOOKS
A Division of Thomas Nelson Publishers
Since 1798

www.thomasnelson.com

Published in Nashville, Tennessee, by Thomas Nelson, Inc.

Scripture quotations noted NKJV are from THE NEW KING JAMES VERSION. Copyright © 1979, 1980, 1982, Thomas Nelson, Inc., Publishers. • Scripture quotations noted GOD'S WORD are from GOD'S WORD, a copyrighted work of God's Word to the Nations Bible Society. Copyright 1995 by God's Word to the Nations Bible Society. All rights reserved. Used by permission. • Scripture quotations noted KJV are from the KING JAMES VERSION. • Scripture quotations noted THE MESSAGE are from *The Message: The New Testament in Contemporary English*. Copyright © 1993, 1994, 1995, 1996, 2000 by Eugene H. Peterson. Used by permission of NavPress Publishing Group. All rights reserved. • Scripture quotations noted NASB are from the NEW AMERICAN STANDARD BIBLE®, © Copyright The Lockman Foundation 1960, 1962, 1963, 1968, 1971, 1972, 1973, 1975, 1977, 1995. Used by permission. • Scripture quotations noted NCV are from the New Century Version®. Copyright © 1987, 1988, 1991 by Word Publishing, a Division of Thomas Nelson, Inc. Used by permission. All rights reserved. • Scripture quotations noted NIV are from the HOLY BIBLE: NEW INTERNATIONAL VERSION®. Copyright © 1973, 1978, 1984 by International Bible Society. Used by permission of Zondervan Publishing House. All rights reserved. • Scripture quotations noted NLT are from the *Holy Bible*, New Living Translation, copyright © 1996. Used by permission of Tyndale House Publishers, Inc., Wheaton, Illinois 60189. All rights reserved. • Scripture quotations noted NRSV are from the NEW REVISED STANDARD VERSION of the Bible. Copyright © 1989 by the Division of Christian Education of the National Council of The Churches of Christ in the U.S.A. All rights reserved.

Managing Editor: Lila Empson

Manuscript written and prepared by Sarah M. Hupp, with contributions from Mary Tucker

Design: Whisner Design Group, Tulsa, Oklahoma

Library of Congress Cataloging-in-Publication Data

Checklist for life for moms : timeless wisdom & foolproof strategies for making the most of life's challenges and opportunities.

   p. cm.

  ISBN 0-7852-6004-8 (pbk.)

  1. Mothers--Religious life. 2. Motherhood--Religious aspects--Christianity. I. Thomas Nelson Publishers.

BV4529.18.C44 2005

248.8'431--dc22

2004028645

Printed in the United States of America

05 06 07 08 CJK 5 4 3 2

Heart Attitude

I will delight in the life
God has given me.

Table of Contents

Table of Contents Continued

Introduction

Having then gifts differing according to the grace that is given to us, let us use them . . . he who leads, with diligence.

ROMANS 12:6, 8 NKJV

Do you ever wish you could have a *Little House on the Prairie* moment? You know the one: Two rocking chairs are pulled up to a fireplace as flames crackle and dance. A grandmother, bent with age, face carved with lines and wrinkles, occupies one chair. In the other rocker you sit expectantly, awaiting words of wisdom. Your child gurgles and coos contentedly in your lap. The hours pass, and you two mothers—one old, one new—share, laugh, and learn all there is to know about mothering. Aah . . .

Unfortunately those tranquil moments exist only on TV. Today's moms live in a reality show of busy days and overscheduled calendars. Probably the only chair you get to occupy for hours on end is the driver's seat of the family car, taking kids to lessons, going to work, running countless other errands. You find yourself pulled in different directions, facing situations for which you feel totally unprepared. Your spiritual life is hit-or-miss, often lost in the never-ending tasks of mothering. You're drowning in responsibilities and would count yourself lucky if you could only tread water.

Take heart, Mom. Whatever your situation, *Checklist for Life for Moms* meets you in the middle of the problems you encounter every day. This unique handbook is built around topics of concern for all moms, bringing a Christian perspective to the ups and downs of mothering. Filled with life-changing principles shared in brief overviews, memorable quotations that will touch your heart, encouraging words from Scripture, and lists that will stretch your mind and spirit, this easily accessible guide will powerfully change your heart and life as you mother your children. You'll also learn creative, practical ways to implement the lessons you've learned, how to share them with your children, and how to help your kids reflect God in their lives, too.

Whether you have an unexpected half-hour or a spare moment while waiting for the next carpool, let *Checklist for Life for Moms* transport you to that longed-for pioneer fireside and find God's wisdom, blessing, and hope with every turn of the page.

God began doing a good work in you, and I am sure he will continue it until it is finished when Jesus Christ comes again.

PHILIPPIANS 1:6 NCV

Children were more to Jesus than helpless, gentle creatures to be loved and protected; they were His chief parable of the kingdom of heaven.

—JOHN WATSON

God always gives his very best to those who leave the choice with him.

JAMES HUDSON TAYLOR

Oh, satisfy us early with Your mercy, that we may rejoice and be glad all our days!

PSALM 90:14 NKJV

As you walk through the valley of the unknown, you will find the footprints of Jesus both in front of you and beside you.

—CHARLES STANLEY

There are only two lasting bequests we can hope to give our children. One of these is roots, the other, wings.

HODDING CARTER

When they see their many children and material blessings, they will recognize the holiness of the Holy One of Israel. They will stand in awe of the God of Israel.

ISAIAH 29:23 NLT

Checklist for Life *for* Moms

There is no power on earth that can neutralize the influence of a high, simple, and useful life.
—Booker T. Washington

Attitude

Positive Polarity

Let this mind be in you, which was also in Christ Jesus.
—PHILIPPIANS 2:5 KJV

Children are fascinated with magnets. Science teaches that when two like ends of magnets are put together, the magnets push each other apart. Conversely, when a positive pole of a magnet is put up against a negative pole of another magnet, the two magnets will stick tightly together.

The powerful, unseen force of your attitude parallels the lessons of a magnet. Like the magnet, if your mind-set or attitude is negatively focused on the negative things about other family members, you'll find your family pushed apart by the polarity of criticism. If your children hear or see only negative words or actions from you about your husband, mother-in-law, or someone at church, your children will push those same people away with their own negative feelings. And if your negative attitude splashes over onto your own children by over-criticizing *their* actions and behavior, you may find your children pushing away from you as well.

Just as magnets have negative and positive poles, so also your attitudes can be positive instead of negative. Actively seeking a positive attitude in negative situations reflects the mind of Christ and helps bring healing to relationships. For example, you may have a poor relationship with your mother-in-law because of past hurts or disagreements. Concentrating on those negatives will only push you farther apart. But if you look for a positive quality in this woman who easily generates such a negative response in you, you may find some common ground or a way to be drawn together.

Remember the Bible story of Jacob and Laban? Though Laban was Jacob's relative, he cheated Jacob over and over again, refusing to give him what he had promised, refusing to pay him what was owed. Yet Jacob didn't say anything bad about Laban. He didn't treat this older man with disrespect. Jacob guarded his thoughts and responded to Laban's negative tricks with hard work and a positive attitude. Genesis 31:7 says that even though Laban cheated Jacob ten times, God did not let Laban's negative ways hurt Jacob at all. Instead Jacob's positive attitude in response to negative conditions brought about unparalleled prosperity for him and his family.

So check your attitude. Be positive. Ask God to help you focus on the positive qualities in those people who might otherwise provoke a negative response, no matter how small those positive qualities may be. Look for common ground, too. Remember, with magnets and relationships, it always takes a positive to grow close to a negative.

I Will

Recognize that my attitudes can have far-reaching effects on my family. _yes_ _no_

Acknowledge that a negative attitude can easily develop into a critical way of life. _yes_ _no_

Accept that I can choose my attitude toward a particular person or situation. _yes_ _no_

Consider that my thoughts and attitudes should reflect those of Christ. _yes_ _no_

Trust God to show me the positive qualities in those who usually engender negative feelings. _yes_ _no_

Appreciate the common ground that can be found in negative or difficult family members. _yes_ _no_

Things to Do

☐ *Play with some magnets while you and your children discuss positive and negative attitudes.*

☐ *Express your pride in your child's accomplishments three times more than you criticize.*

☐ *Take the emphasis off correcting and disciplining. Look instead for ways to compliment and encourage.*

☐ *Watch yourself in a mirror saying positive things. Remember your reflection when tempted to be negative.*

☐ *Read Luke 6:37–42 with your children. Discuss how judging others can affect your attitudes.*

☐ *Play the game of opposites with your kids. For every negative, think of a positive: Bad/Good, Sad/Happy, Mean/Nice.*

Things to Remember

Watch over your heart with all diligence, for from it flow the springs of life.

PROVERBS 4:23 NASB

What does the LORD require of you but to do justly, to love mercy, and to walk humbly with your God?

MICAH 6:8 NKJV

There must be a spiritual renewal of your thoughts and attitudes. You must display a new nature.

EPHESIANS 4:23–24 NLT

Let the teaching of Christ live in you richly. . . . Everything you do or say should be done to obey Jesus your Lord.

COLOSSIANS 3:16–17 NCV

I try to please everybody in every way. For I am not seeking my own good but the good of many, so that they may be saved.

1 CORINTHIANS 10:33 NIV

Here is a simple, rule-of-thumb guide for behavior: Ask yourself what you want people to do for you, then grab the initiative and do it for them.

MATTHEW 7:11 THE MESSAGE

There is little difference in people, but that little difference makes a big difference. That little difference is attitude. The big difference is whether it is positive or negative.

—CLEMENT STONE

Circumstances and situations do color life, but you have been given the mind to choose what the color shall be.

—JOHN HOMER MILLER

Listening

I Can't Hear You

Men listened to me and waited, and kept silence for my counsel.

—Job 29:21 NKJV

"Did you hear me?" "Were you listening to me?" You've probably asked your children these questions more times than you care to count. Your children may have resorted to more physical means to get you to listen to them—draping themselves over your body, hanging from every appendage, endlessly repeating, "Mommy! Mommy!"

Listening is tough work. It takes time, concentration, and interest. Listening involves centering your focus on an individual and opening your mind *and ears* to what is being said. Quality listening affirms the value of each individual and makes families and relationships stronger. So, how can you show you care by listening better?

First you may need to unlearn some bad habits. Maybe you usually talk first and listen last. Why not try a new one-two punch? Try listening first and talking last. Maybe you're usually trying to do two things at the same time—listening *and* . . . listening and folding the laundry, listening and washing the dishes, listening and paying the bills. Try stopping what you're doing when a child wants to talk to you or suggesting getting together in just a minute so that you can give your child your full attention. Maybe you need a physical cue to remind yourself to shift your focus from doing to listening. Take a deep breath; close your eyes for a second; sit down.

To get your children to listen to you, you may need to try new communication techniques. When God met with Elijah in 1 Kings 19, Elijah experienced the noise of a whirlwind, an earthquake, and a roaring fire. Yet it wasn't until after the fire that God began to speak with Elijah in "a still small voice" (1 Kings 19:12 KJV). If you've been a shoutin' Momma, noisily whirling words and shaking the rafters to communicate, follow God's example. To get your kids listening, try whispering.

Then work together with your children on active listening skills. Face the person you're listening or speaking to. Look him or her in the eye. Ask questions like "How do you feel about that?" to understand what someone is trying to tell you. For assurance that you're really hearing what is being said, summarize what you hear in your own words. Say something like "What I hear you saying is . . ." Your active listening will show your children that they are important to you. And, by actively listening to your children when they speak to you, they'll learn (hopefully) to be better listeners themselves, too.

I Will

Recognize the value of developing the skill of listening.

yes *no*

Ask forgiveness when I fail to listen to God and my children.

yes *no*

Understand it's important to use my ears more than I use my lips.

yes *no*

Consider my words and tone when I want my children to listen to me.

yes *no*

Acknowledge that being intent on giving advice means I may miss hearing what is being said.

yes *no*

Keep my heart and mind open to truly listening to my children instead of multitasking while they're talking.

yes *no*

Things to Do

- [ ] *Devise a family signal—a whistle or hand clap—as a reminder to be quiet and listen.*

- [ ] *To develop listening skills in younger kids, tell stories about when they were born.*

- [ ] *Take your children to the park and listen. How many different sounds can you identify?*

- [ ] *Start a story with your kids as the heroes. Listen as they finish the tale.*

- [ ] *Inquire about school activities each day. Listen carefully to their problems and feelings.*

- [ ] *Hide under the covers with your kids and listen to their bedtime prayers.*

Things to Remember

Come here and listen to me! I'll pour out the spirit of wisdom upon you and make you wise.

PROVERBS 1:23 NLT

If you listen to correction to improve your life, you will live among the wise.

PROVERBS 15:31 NCV

Be careful how you listen. Those who have understanding will be given more. But those who do not have understanding, even what they think they have will be taken away from them.

LUKE 8:18 NCV

We must pay more careful attention, therefore, to what we have heard, so that we do not drift away.

HEBREWS 2:1 NIV

Hear, my child, your father's instruction, and do not reject your mother's teaching; for they are a fair garland for your head, and pendants for your neck.

PROVERBS 1:8–9 NRSV

My sheep listen to my voice; I know them, and they follow me. I give them eternal life, and they shall never perish.

JOHN 10:27–28 NIV

One of the best ways to persuade others is with your ears—by listening to them.

—DEAN RUSK

While the right to talk may be the beginning of freedom, the necessity of listening is what makes the right important.

—WALTER LIPPMANN

Godly Confidence

I Know We Can

The Lord will be your confidence.

—Proverbs 3:26 NKJV

Some experienced moms never seem to be overwhelmed, no matter the situation. Yet for new moms who have little experience in mothering, holding a baby is enough of a challenge, let alone being totally responsible for a child's every need. *Doesn't this baby come with a how-to manual?* they wonder. Even if a child came with an instruction manual, a mom can't hold a child with one hand and keep her place in the how-to book with the other. In order to survive, moms need to possess an inner confidence.

Where does this confidence come from? Many psychologists preach, "You can do anything. Just trust in yourself." Accepting this rhetoric, many moms sound like the little engine in the children's storybook, puffing up the hill saying, "I think I can; I think I can." Unfortunately, being human means you have limitations. You'll be able to do some things, but not others. Because of these limitations, moms need to base their inner confidence on something better than self. To raise children in today's world, moms need to depend on God in every mothering situation. Moms need to change their thoughts from *I think I can* to *I know God can.*

Consider this. Mathew 5:48 says that God is perfect. Everything God does, says, creates, or sustains contains no errors, no mistakes. That includes choosing you as a mother. God has given you to your child because there is no other mom on the planet that could be as good a mother to your child as you can be. God made you and knows your strengths and weaknesses better than you do. With God by your side, you can do a good job mothering your child.

Trust God—that's the first step to becoming a confident mother. Tell God your concerns about being a good mom. Then follow the example of Jesus' mother, Mary. When an angel told her she would bear God's Son, Mary was a bit overwhelmed but replied in faith, "I am the servant of the Lord. Let this happen to me as you say!" (Luke 1:38 NCV). Surrender to God's will as Mary did, believing, "God has chosen me to mother this child. I know He has."

God has also given moms two invaluable confidence builders to depend upon—godly mentors and His guidance. The little engine in that children's storybook ran along two railroad tracks to keep it going in the right direction. The twin rails of godly mentors and God's guidance can counsel you, keep you from making wrong choices, and send you in the right direction of confident mothering. Seek out a Christian mom or grandmother who has raised her children or grandchildren well. Watch her as she interacts with the children in her life. Ask her for some friendly advice. And recognize that you might be able to help an even younger mother with some mothering suggestions. Titus 2:3–5 says when older, godly women help younger women learn to care for their families, everyone benefits.

The second rail of the railroad track to inner confidence is God's guidance found through prayer and Bible study. Prayer brings your need to be a good mom into focus, while God's Word reassures you that God will give you the strength and ability to accomplish whatever He asks of you. God's Word contains everything from parenting tips to ways to surmount overwhelming situations. Search the Scriptures for these instructions. Ask God to guide you as you begin to use His parenting guidelines with your family.

When it comes to mothering, toss the I-think-I-can pop-culture idea into the diaper pail. Know instead that God has chosen you to be your child's mother, that godly mentors can help give advice you need to be a great mom, and that God will guide you in every situation. Relax and let God work in and through you to make you the mom your children need. Together you and God can face anything. Your inner confidence, when built on God's strength, will change that little engine's tune from I-think-I-can to I-know-God-and-I-can.

I Will

Recognize that real confidence is found in trusting God.   _yes_   _no_

Ask for God's guidance to help me raise my children.   _yes_   _no_

Remember that no mom is perfect, including me, despite my best intentions.   _yes_   _no_

Carefully consider and carry out the principles in God's Word for raising children.   _yes_   _no_

Watch and learn from other godly moms.   _yes_   _no_

Pray for my children individually each day.   _yes_   _no_

Things to Do

☐ Make a list of your strengths and weaknesses as a mother.

☐ Memorize Philippians 4:13 and thank God for helping you to be a good mom.

☐ Seek out a godly mom or grandmother to mentor you.

☐ Write the words "I know God can" on a picture of a locomotive.

☐ Search God's Word for three parenting tips you can use in your family.

☐ Offer your friendship to a less experienced mom and begin sharing mothering hints together.

☐ Tell a friend how God is making you a more confident mom.

Things to Remember

You have been my hope, O Sovereign LORD, my confidence since my youth. From birth I have relied on you; you brought me forth from my mother's womb. I will ever praise you.

PSALM 71:5–6 NIV

Blessed are those who trust in the Lord and have made the Lord their hope and confidence.

JEREMIAH 17:7 NLT

He said to me, "My grace is sufficient for you, for My strength is made perfect in weakness."
2 Corinthians 12:9 NKJV

Do not throw away this confident trust in the Lord, no matter what happens. Remember the great reward it brings you!

HEBREWS 10:35 NLT

Not that we are sufficient of ourselves to think of anything as being from ourselves, but our sufficiency is from God.

2 CORINTHIANS 3:5 NKJV

Let us draw near with confidence to the throne of grace, that we may receive mercy and find grace to help in time of need.

HEBREWS 4:16 NASB

He alone is my rock and my salvation;
he is my fortress, I will never be shaken.

PSALM 62:2 NIV

Blessed is the person who places his
confidence in the LORD and does not
rely on arrogant people.

PSALM 40:4 GOD'S WORD

This is the confidence that we have in
Him, that if we ask anything according
to His will, He hears us.

1 JOHN 5:14 NKJV

The work of righteousness will be peace,
And the service of righteousness,
quietness and confidence forever.

ISAIAH 32:17 NASB

In the fear of the LORD there is strong
confidence, and his children will have a
place of refuge.

PROVERBS 14:26 GOD'S WORD

I can do everything with the help of
Christ who gives me the strength I need.

PHILIPPIANS 4:13 NLT

**Without the
assistance of that
Divine Being I
cannot succeed;
with that
assistance I
cannot fail.**

—ABRAHAM LINCOLN

**'Twant me, 'twas
the Lord. I always
told him, "I trust
to you. I don't
know where to go
or what to do, but
I expect you to
lead me," and he
always did.**

—HARRIET TUBMAN

Kids and School

Give 'Em a Break

Study to shew thyself approved unto God.

—2 Timothy 2:15 KJV

Researchers and educators agree: Schools are in trouble. Classrooms are overcrowded; programs are underfunded. Shorter school days, outdated materials, and inadequate supplies of textbooks, computers, and other materials make teaching and learning difficult. Yet the greatest problem facing teachers today isn't the growing lack of resources. It's the age-old problem of parental opposition.

Think about it. Every complaint you utter against your child's teacher falls on your kids' receptive ears, sprouting into classroom problems and disrespectful attitudes. After all, how bright could any teacher be who assigns "too much homework" or who's "always picking on my child"? A mom who passes these types of complaints on to her children is also liable to accept as utter truth her child's criticism, "That teacher is always picking on me" or "That teacher just assigns things without telling us how to do them" or, the most common, "I'm flunking because that teacher doesn't know how to teach." God's Word is clear: "Do all things without complaining and disputing" (Philippians 2:14 NKJV). Give teachers a break. Close down the complaint office. Keep your comments to yourself until you can voice them personally in a parent-teacher conference (no children allowed, please).

Then, to foster a better learning environment, work with teachers, not against them. Remember teachers are human, just like you are. They have good days and bad days, just like you do. So make sure your kids are doing their homework, reading their assignments, studying for their tests. Remember, there are always two sides to every story that junior brings home from school. Give teachers a chance to prove that they're not the two-headed monsters your children say they are.

In addition, help your child do better in school by instilling a love of learning. Explore museums and historical sites. Use the Internet to research items of interest from ants to Antarctica. Encourage a love for books and reading. Rest your weary bones, place a small child on your lap, and read aloud every day. Let your budding scholars read aloud to you, too, as you wash dishes or sort laundry. Motivate your kids to read from books on different subjects by different authors. Make sure each child has a library card. Let the treats for good behavior at the doctor's office or grocery store be noncaloric, tooth-healthy books. Reading will help your children learn about language—sentence structure, punctuation, grammar, vocabulary—and open their eyes to the wonders of God's world, too.

I Will

Acknowledge that my attitudes about school, homework, and teachers can affect my children's attitudes, too. _____ yes _____ no

Rely on God to daily help me criticize less and praise more. _____ yes _____ no

Consider that my children and their teachers will have good days and bad days. _____ yes _____ no

Seek to verify the details of teacher-child disputes before taking action. _____ yes _____ no

Actively look for ways to help my child become a better student. _____ yes _____ no

Things to Do

☐ *Become a volunteer at school in the library, lunchroom, playground, or on a school committee.*

☐ *Pray with children before they study for tests, asking God to help them remember things.*

☐ *Set aside a daily study time for your children to work on homework together.*

☐ *Turn off the radio, television, and telephone for serious study during homework time.*

☐ *Visit your child's classroom during an average school day to watch teacher-student interaction.*

☐ *Schedule a family forum to ask your kids what worries them about school.*

Things to Remember

Let the wise listen and add to their learning, and let the discerning get guidance.

PROVERBS 1:5 NIV

Lazy people want much but get little, but those who work hard will prosper and be satisfied.

PROVERBS 13:4 NLT

Study this Book of the Law continually. Meditate on it day and night so you may be sure to obey all that is written in it. Only then will you succeed.

JOSHUA 1:8 NLT

Truly happy people are those who carefully study God's perfect law that makes people free, and they continue to study it. They do not forget what they heard.

JAMES 1:25 NCV

The good hand of his God was upon him. For Ezra had set his heart to study the law of the LORD and to practice it.

EZRA 7:9–10 NASB

A student is not better than the teacher, but the student who has been fully trained will be like the teacher.

LUKE 6:40 NCV

If a man empties his purse into his head no one can take it away from him. An investment in knowledge always pays the best interest.

—BENJAMIN FRANKLIN

Every child must be encouraged to get as much education as he has the ability to take . . . Nothing matters more to the future of our country.

—LYNDON B. JOHNSON

Friendship

Openhearted Folks

A despairing man should have the devotion of his friends.
—Job 6:14 NIV

    The phone rings; you pick up the receiver. When you hear the caller's voice, it doesn't matter that it's the middle of the night. Your friend is on the line, and when a friend has a need, sleep can wait. That's the power of friendship. And that's how God made you, too.

    God created you and your kids to be social beings. All people, regardless of age, need friends—openhearted folks who touch their lives. When tiny babies or toddlers catch sight of other little ones, they'll make eye contact, babble at each other, or try to touch one another. By the time children are three years old, they'll even play together for a short time without fighting as long as they have enough toys or don't have to share the ones they do have for very long.

    Learning to make friends is as important to your child's development as learning to count from one to ten. Little ones often form their first friendships with other children who live in their neighborhood or attend their church. These children become your kids' friends because they are available. You can expand your child's group of friends by taking part in church school classes, sports programs, or weekly play dates in the park. By the time your child is three years old, nursery school may open another avenue for friendships. At this age children begin to prefer one friend over another, just as they prefer one color of crayon over another. Use wisdom and ask other children to visit and play, too, so that your child will learn to make friends with new people. This skill will help your kids as they mature; they won't feel threatened in a roomful of unfamiliar faces.

Children learn important lessons from friends about relationships, so before your kids are school-age teach them how to choose good friends. Encourage them to look for honesty, kindness, dependability, good judgment, and godliness. Stay involved in the friendship process, too. Make your home a fun place for kids to gather. Be open, pleasant, and observant. Though some of your children's friends might have different values than you do, don't make disapproving comments. If you notice a potential problem with a friend, ask your child questions about that friend, expressing your unease by focusing on the friend's well-being.

God wants you and your kids to be openhearted people who bless and encourage others with hope and love. That's what friends do—even in the middle of the night.

I Will

Be thankful to God for my friends.		*yes*	*no*
Make finding good friends a high priority in my kids' lives.		*yes*	*no*
Trust God to use friends to help me and my children grow in many ways.		*yes*	*no*
Ask God to show my children and me how to be better friends to others.		*yes*	*no*
Look for ways to make my home a friendly place.		*yes*	*no*
Pray for my children to make wise decisions in choosing their friends.		*yes*	*no*

Things to Do

☐ *Celebrate. Throw a party for adults and kids just to say thanks for being friends.*

☐ *Print Matthew 12:33 under a picture of fruit trees. Label the fruit with friendship traits.*

☐ *Find pictures of people your kids would like as friends. Discuss reasons for their choices.*

☐ *Invite a new child from school or church to play at your house one afternoon.*

☐ *Read 1 Samuel 20:1–42. List the ways Jonathan was a good friend to David.*

☐ *Plan an outing with a church family whose kids are the same age as yours.*

Things to Remember

Perfume and incense bring joy to the heart, and the pleasantness of one's friend springs from his earnest counsel.

PROVERBS 27:9 NIV

A friend loves at all times, and a brother is born for adversity.

PROVERBS 17:17 NKJV

Friendship with the LORD is reserved for those who fear him. With them he shares the secrets of his covenant.

PSALM 25:14 NLT

Never abandon a friend—either yours or your father's. Then in your time of need, you won't have to ask your relatives for assistance. It is better to go to a neighbor than to a relative who lives far away.

PROVERBS 27:10 NLT

Greater love has no one than this, than to lay down one's life for his friends.

JOHN 15:13 NKJV

Some friends play at friendship but a true friend sticks closer than one's nearest kin.

PROVERBS 18:24 NRSV

A true friend shares freely, advises justly, assists readily, adventures boldly, takes all patiently, defends courageously, and continues a friend unchangeably.

—WILLIAM PENN

There are deep sorrows and killing cares in life, but the encouragement and love of friends were given us to make all difficulties bearable.

—JOHN OLIVER HOBBES

Adoption

Another Option

---

*You should behave . . . like God's very own children, adopted
into his family—calling him "Father, dear Father."*

—ROMANS 8:15 NLT

Stuart Little, a popular children's movie, traces the
misadventures of a family who adopts a mouse named Stuart
to be their son. Initially the family cat believes Stuart is
nothing more than a tasty midnight snack. George, the Littles'
natural son, finds nothing in common with this pint-sized,
other-species sibling. Yet, by bearing the family's name,
exhibiting the family's courage, and carrying on the family's
traditions, Stuart becomes more than an adoptee. At book's
end he is an accepted and loved member of the family.

While Stuart's experience is fiction, the process of
adoption is very real. Families have been opening their hearts
and homes to others for centuries. God's Word records the
story of Pharaoh's daughter, whose heart broke for a helpless
baby boy. She adopted Moses as her son, giving him life when
it seemed his existence was doomed. The apostle Paul also
reminds us that God offers spiritual adoption into His family
for anyone who believes on His name.

Today many children of all ages and nationalities are awaiting adoption, praying for a new life with a real family. If you feel an inner tug on your heart when you think of children without families, God may be nudging you to become an adoptive mom. Adoption is just another way for a child to be born into your family. Though that child may not look like you physically, she will one day think and act like you and value what you value because she will be *your* child, nurtured by you.

So do some homework. Ask God for His guidance as you begin looking at the adoption options. Question adoption agencies and families who have adopted children. Attend an adoption workshop at your church or community center. Learn all you can. If that nudge to adopt is still there, trust God and go for it. Begin the formal adoption process and give a child an opportunity for a new life.

There are some informal adoption options, too. In our society many children do not have the benefit of extended family. Distance separates many grandparents and grandchildren. Some children also long for the safety and acceptance of a surrogate mom—someone who will listen to their fears and encourage their ideas. Children with these needs may live in your neighborhood or attend your church. By volunteering your time as a substitute mom or grandmom, you could touch the lives of these children in wonderful ways. The adoption options are endless. Maybe one is just right for you.

I Will

Gratefully praise God for adopting me and loving me as His child.

    yes   *no*

Believe that choosing to love someone outside my natural family can be an enriching experience.

    yes   *no*

Be thankful for those who touched my life as surrogate moms and grandmoms.

    yes   *no*

Rely on God to work through me to favorably touch the lives of other children.

    yes   *no*

Remember to pray for children and families going through the adoption process.

    yes   *no*

Consider how limited a child's life can be without a real family.

    yes   *no*

Things to Do

☐ *Attend an adoption seminar or workshop at your church or community center.*

☐ *Interview an adoptive parent to learn about the adoption process.*

☐ *Make certificates for you and your children to commemorate your adoption into God's family.*

☐ *Check out adoption agencies by researching them online or visiting their offices in person.*

☐ *Investigate foster care programs available in your county; foster parenting often leads to adoption.*

☐ *Find a lonesome child at your church. Offer to be an extra mom or grandmom.*

Things to Remember

When at last they had to abandon him, Pharaoh's daughter found him and raised him as her own son.

ACTS 7:21 NLT

Hadassah was also called Esther. Mordecai had adopted her as his own daughter when her father and mother died.

ESTHER 2:7 NCV

Because of his love, God had already decided to make us his own children through Jesus Christ. That was what he wanted and what pleased him.

EPHESIANS 1:5 NCV

God sent him to buy freedom for us who were slaves to the law, so that he could adopt us as his very own children.

GALATIANS 4:5 NLT

You are not a slave; you are God's child, and God will give you the blessing he promised, because you are his child.

GALATIANS 4:7 NCV

We also who have the firstfruits of the Spirit, even we ourselves groan within ourselves, eagerly waiting for the adoption, the redemption of our body.

ROMANS 8:23 NKJV

Children are not casual guests in our home. They have been loaned to us temporarily for the purpose of loving them.

—JAMES C. DOBSON

It is the great privilege which believers have through Christ that they are adopted children of the God of heaven. We who by nature are children of wrath and disobedience have become by grace children of love.

—MATTHEW HENRY

Prayer

Conversations with God

Pray without ceasing. —1 THESSALONIANS 5:17 KJV

Doctors are consistent in their advice to moms who want to be healthy: Get more exercise. Vacuuming and housework, gardening and grocery shopping, chasing after children and folding laundry all burn calories, but a regular regimen of aerobic and anaerobic exercise is needed for strong bones and muscles. In the same way, God's Word is consistent in its advice to moms who want to be spiritually healthy: Pray more. Prayer is an exercise for your spirit. Bowing your head and bending your knees in prayer will build up the muscles of your faith.

You've probably already begun this soul-building exercise program without knowing it. You might have taught your children to bow their heads, fold their hands, and close their eyes when they pray. Closed eyes help children focus their attention on God. Folded hands and bowed heads teach kids that God deserves respect and reverence, too. But the important thing about prayer is not a physical prayer posture. The key to all prayer is the desire of a heart to communicate with God, for prayer is a conversation with God.

Prayer is more than a formal exercise or recitation in church, too. In fact, you don't have to be in church to talk to God. You can talk to Him anywhere, at anytime. You don't have to be on your knees with your hands folded; you don't have to close your eyes. Some of your best prayer times can be when you're alone in your car or taking the commuter train home from work. Wherever you are, whatever you're doing, if you can think, you can pray.

Remember, too, that muscle mass isn't obvious after one day of exercise, nor will your faith and spirit grow with only a few prayers. To see the spirit-building effects of prayer, pray and then pray some more. You may be tempted to give up, to think that praying about your situations and concerns won't do any good. But keep at it. God's Word assures you that God wants to hear from you. He promises to answer your prayers, too.

You can pour out your heart to Him, ask Him for help, praise Him for who He is, thank Him for what He has done for you, confess your sin to Him and ask for forgiveness, tell Him your needs, even share your feelings of anger or discouragement. Talking to God about all these things will stretch your trust and flex your faith.

As a mother you have plenty to pray about for your children, too. Children are very direct with their needs. If something hurts, they howl. If they're hungry, they say so. So be like a little child in your prayers. Be direct. Be honest. When you're almost out of patience with a terrible two, ask for more. When your kids disobey and disappoint you, take your frustration to God. When you know your kids need help beyond your ability, commit them into God's hands. When your teenager pushes your buttons and you to the edge, ask for wisdom and compassion. And, when your kids make you proud, share your joy with God. Don't give up on prayer. A lack of prayer forms a flabby faith and leaves you defenseless, without God's presence when you need it most. Keep your faith muscle strong—pray.

Begin the day with God. Talk to Him before your feet hit the floor. Ask Him to guide you, to use you and your children. Speak with Him often throughout the day. Nothing is too insignificant to mention. Remember, too, that Jesus prayed for you long before you were born, praying that God's love would be in you, that you would be unified with other believers, that you would find joy and be protected from evil. End each day thanking God for these things and for His never-ending care. Let your children know that you have constant conversations with God and that you pray for them often. Encourage them to pray, too. Then watch for the difference prayer makes in your attitudes and relationships. You'll be amazed at the flexibility of your faith, the strength of your spirit. The exercise of prayer really does change things.

I Will

Believe that God wants to hear what I
have to say.

yes _no_
_____ _____

Talk to God about my children every day.

yes _no_
_____ _____

Encourage my children to pray on their own
at all times.

yes _no_
_____ _____

Watch for God's answers to my prayers and
thank Him.

yes _no_
_____ _____

Remember to pray at all times—angry, helpless,
joyful, frustrated, peaceful, happy, or sad.

yes _no_
_____ _____

Things to Do

☐ *Find prayers in the Psalms that you can pray together with your
children.*

☐ *Tell a friend about a prayer God has answered for you.*

☐ *Schedule a time to pray with your children about their requests.*

☐ *Make a list of people your family will pray for together this week.*

☐ *Learn a chorus or hymn about prayer to sing with your children.*

☐ *Print MAKE TIME TO TALK TO GOD. Post this reminder under your kitchen
clock.*

☐ *Read Daniel 6 with your children. Discuss Daniel's prayer life
and its results.*

Things to Remember

Confess your sins to each other and pray for each other so God can heal you. When a believing person prays, great things happen.

JAMES 5:16 NCV

Is any one of you in trouble? He should pray. Is anyone happy? Let him sing songs of praise.

JAMES 5:13 NIV

The eyes of the LORD are on the righteous, and His ears are open to their prayers.

1 PETER 3:12 NKJV

I call on you, O God, for you will answer me;
give ear to me and hear my prayer.
Psalm 17:6 NIV

The LORD detests the sacrifice of the wicked, but the prayer of the upright pleases him.

PROVERBS 15:8 NIV

When you pray, I will listen. If you look for me in earnest, you will find me when you seek me.

JEREMIAH 29:12–13 NLT

I tell you that if two of you on earth agree about something and pray for it, it will be done for you by my Father in heaven.

MATTHEW 18:19 NCV

Whatever we ask we receive from Him, because we keep His commandments and do those things that are pleasing in His sight.

1 JOHN 3:22 NKJV

When you pray, go into your room, and when you have shut your door, pray to your Father who is in the secret place.

MATTHEW 6:6 KJV

Pray in the Spirit at all times with all kinds of prayers, asking for everything you need. To do this you must always be ready and never give up.

EPHESIANS 6:18 NCV

All who obey you should pray to you while they still can. When troubles rise like a flood, they will not reach them.

PSALM 32:6 NCV

Until now you have asked nothing in My name. Ask, and you will receive, that your joy may be full.

JOHN 16:24 NKJV

When we pray, it is far more important to pray with a sense of the greatness of God than with a sense of the greatness of the problem.

—EVANGELINE BLOOD

Men may spurn our appeals, reject our message, oppose our arguments, despise our persons—but they are helpless against our prayers.

—J. SIDLOW BAXTER

Lifestyle Changes

More Difficult Than Diapers

There is a time to tear apart and a time to sew together.
—ECCLESIASTES 3:7 NCV

Change a diaper; change the sheets; change your underwear. Some changes in life are easy for moms and kids to handle. But lifestyle changes are more difficult. Losing a job is tough. Relocating from one city to another is daunting. Dissolving a marriage through death, divorce, or separation triggers unbearable stress. Moving elderly relatives from their home into yours causes friction. In situations like these moms and children can feel torn apart at the seams.

To sew your family back together, remember that God knows what you're going through. Be honest as you pray for His help, strength, and wisdom. Seek out a pastor or another godly mom. Share your hurts with him; ask for her advice; solicit his or her prayers.

If you have to move, realize you're not alone. Statistics indicate 20 percent of American families move every year. Read the story of Jacob in Genesis 28:10–21. Forced to leave home for an uncertain future, Jacob was assured in a dream of God's presence with him. You can assure your children that God will be with you as you move, too. Make them a part of the process. Focus on the adventure of going to a new place, not on the sadness of leaving the old. If possible, visit your new surroundings before you move to familiarize your children with their new school, the churches nearby, and the activities available for leisure times.

If your family has experienced a change in marital status due to divorce or separation, reassure your children they did not cause the family breakup. Assure them that you and your spouse still love them and will care for them. If possible, let the custodial parent keep the children in the family home. Familiar surroundings will help your children cope with change. If an untimely death takes a spouse from the family, seek grief counseling for you and your child. If an elderly relative now calls your home theirs, too, find ways to offer them privacy. Arrange for separate telephone lines and televisions. But enfold these folks into your daily routines, too. Maybe they could fix supper occasionally or be the bedtime storyteller.

In all of life's changes, God has promised to work out everything for good. As you begin each day, remember the phrase from God's Word, "It came to pass." Let that phrase remind you that though life's changes may seem overwhelming, your situation, too, will pass. And the next change on the horizon might just bring about something better.

I Will

Understand that major changes in life happen to everyone. ___yes___ ___no___

Acknowledge that God is always with me even when I'm going through a major life change. ___yes___ ___no___

Endeavor to look at my lifestyle changes with a positive attitude. ___yes___ ___no___

Keep my negative feelings about others who might have caused this change to myself. ___yes___ ___no___

Remember that God has promised to work out everything for my good. ___yes___ ___no___

Trust God for His continuing care throughout life's major changes. ___yes___ ___no___

Things to Do

- [ ] *Ask your kids to draw pictures about a major change facing your family. Talk about their concerns.*

- [ ] *To keep family ties strong during lifestyle changes, institute a monthly family night to watch videos.*

- [ ] *Go through old papers, books, and memorabilia. Throw away things that stir up bad feelings.*

- [ ] *With your kids, change their bed sheets. Talk about changes, both big and small.*

- [ ] *Play the games of Monopoly or Life to give kids a fun way to experience lifestyle changes.*

- [ ] *Take turns making up a story. Swap storytellers by saying, "and it came to pass . . ."*

Things to Remember

Jesus Christ is the same yesterday, today, and forever. So do not be attracted by strange, new ideas. Your spiritual strength comes from God's special favor.

HEBREWS 13:8–9 NLT

I am the LORD, I do not change; therefore you are not consumed, O sons of Jacob.

MALACHI 3:6 NKJV

Every good action and every perfect gift is from God. These good gifts come down from the Creator of the sun, moon, and stars, who does not change like their shifting shadows.

JAMES 1:17 NCV

God is not a man, that he should lie, nor a son of man, that he should change his mind. Does he speak and then not act? Does he promise and not fulfill?

NUMBERS 23:19 NIV

He who is the Glory of Israel does not lie or change his mind; for he is not a man, that he should change his mind.

1 SAMUEL 15:29 NIV

Do not call to mind the former things, or ponder things of the past. Behold, I will do something new, now it will spring forth.

ISAIAH 43:18–19 NASB

If we try to resist loss and change or to hold on to blessings and joy belonging to a past which must drop away from us, we postpone all the new blessings awaiting us.

—HANNAH HURNARD

"And this, too, shall pass away." How much it expresses! How chastening in the hour of pride! How consoling in the depths of affliction!

—ABRAHAM LINCOLN

Beauty

Downright Ugly Ducklings

He has made everything beautiful in its time.

—ECCLESIASTES 3:11 NKJV

In the fable *The Ugly Duckling,* a swan's egg gets mixed up in a nest of duck eggs. When the hatchlings emerge, the baby swan is so different from the baby ducks everyone says it's ugly. The fable ends as the swan's true identity is discovered. The unusual hatchling might have been ugly by duck standards, but it is beautiful to other swans, for beauty *is* found in the eye of the beholder—whether you're a duck, a swan, or a person.

God's Word takes the lesson of this story one step further. God wants your beauty to be more than what's apparent on the outside. God wants the hidden person of your heart to be beautiful, too, with "the incorruptible beauty of a gentle and quiet spirit" (1 Peter 3:4 KJV). Asking forgiveness for an ugly remark made in anger, erasing mean feelings you've harbored about someone, or replacing bad attitudes with godly ones are all ways to bring beauty to the inner you.

Kids need a dose of inner beautification, too. After all, kids are the ones who come up with ugly nicknames for siblings who don't play fair. Kids are swift to point out your faults. And kids can be cruel to others with cutting remarks or bullying tactics. So start your kids on some heart changes by teaching them to think first and speak second, reminding them to treat others as they want to be treated.

Outward beauty is an issue for kids, too. There are times when a child may feel ugly and say so. If this happens, ask questions to determine the reason for negative remarks. Is weight a problem? What is it about your child's feet, nose, or ears that seems too big or small? Did someone make a comment about him or her? Consider what's going on in your child's life. Is there a reason for increased anxiety? Is school picture day coming up? Maybe a new hairstyle, contact lenses, braces, or a workout program could remedy the perceived "ugly" problem.

Finally, consider what your child's friends do to look good. Just because someone else wears tattoos, body piercings, a push-up bra, or makeup doesn't mean your child needs these to look that kind of good, too. Discuss together your family's standards and age limits for these things. And remember: there will always be bad hair days, days when you all feel like downright ugly ducklings. But God sees the swans hiding inside all ugly ducklings. You're always beautiful to Him, because He makes *everything* beautiful.

I Will

Remember that beauty is found in eye of
the beholder.

yes _____ _no_ _____

Believe that God always finds me beautiful—even
on bad hair days.

yes _____ _no_ _____

Actively seek to find the inner beauty of a gentle
and quiet spirit.

yes _____ _no_ _____

Realize that treating others like I want to be
treated is one way to beautify my spirit.

yes _____ _no_ _____

Help my children turn their ugly duckling attitudes
to beautiful, godly ones.

yes _____ _no_ _____

Ask God to show me ways to calm my child's
beauty anxieties.

yes _____ _no_ _____

Things to Do

☐ _Buy or make something beautiful for each member of your family to wear._

☐ _Let your kids draw a cartoon panel of_ The Ugly Duckling _to remember no one's ugly._

☐ _Ask God to resolve three ugly things that have impaired your spirit—anger, unforgiveness, and stubbornness._

☐ _Donate a used prom dress to the Salvation Army so someone else can look beautiful on prom night._

☐ _Ask a friend to help you find a flattering hairstyle to boost your outward beauty._

☐ _Examine a pretty rock with your kids. Discuss how its imperfections add to its beauty._

Things to Remember

Do not let your adornment be merely outward—arranging the hair, wearing gold, or putting on fine apparel—rather let it be the hidden person of the heart, with the incorruptible beauty of a gentle and quiet spirit.

1 PETER 3:3–4 NKJV

Charm is deceptive, and beauty does not last; but a woman who fears the LORD will be greatly praised.

PROVERBS 31:30 NLT

The LORD takes pleasure in His people; He will beautify the humble with salvation.

PSALM 149:4 NKJV

To all who mourn in Israel, he will give beauty for ashes, joy instead of mourning, praise instead of despair.

ISAIAH 61:3 NLT

Oh yes! GOD gives Goodness and Beauty; our land responds with Bounty and Blessing. Right Living strides out before him, and clears a path for his passage.

PSALM 85:12–13 THE MESSAGE

Give to the LORD the glory due His name; bring an offering, and come before Him. Oh, worship the LORD in the beauty of holiness!

1 CHRONICLES 16:29 NKJV

The beautiful is a phenomenon which is never apparent of itself, but is reflected in a thousand different works of the Creator.

—JOHANN WOLFGANG VON GOETHE

Characteristics which define beauty are wholeness, harmony, and radiance.

—SAINT THOMAS AQUINAS

Anger

Deal with It

Cease from anger, and forsake wrath; do not fret—it only causes harm. —PSALM 37:8 NKJV

Stacy had been asking the children at the pajama party to quiet down for almost an hour, but the noise just kept getting louder. With each passing moment Stacy's irritation grew, until finally she shrieked an ultimatum that quieted the gathering but blanketed her household with embarrassment.

A week later Stacy and her children attended the annual church picnic. The pastor wanted to quiet the gathering to pray, but no one seemed to hear him. Stacy anxiously watched the situation, noting the pastor's mounting frustration. Then, just for the briefest of seconds, the pastor bowed his head. Immediately a choir member touched his elbow. Together the two began to sing, barely being heard over the noise of the picnic revelers. As Stacy watched, others began to join the pastor in song. By the end of the hymn all the picnic participants were singing together. In the hushed moment of the hymn's *Amen,* the pastor offered his prayer for the meal.

Stacy learned some important lessons at that picnic. Watching her pastor, Stacy realized that harmful anger often begins with something small, growing from the embers of irritation and frustration, or finding root in jealousy, envy, and hurtful words. If these things show up at your house, remind yourself they don't have to be invited in and allowed to grow into anger. You can choose to stop them at the door. Follow the pastor's example and pray. Stacy's pastor later confided that he *was* getting frustrated about the picnic noise, but he took his feelings to God instead of allowing anger to grow. And, the pastor added, no sooner had he prayed than the choir member suggested singing as a means of quieting the group. If you, too, flood the growing fires of anger with the peace of prayer, God will show you a constructive way handle it.

Note also in Stacy's situations that the longer that time elapsed before the irritation was resolved, the more chance it had to grow into anger. Short-circuiting troublesome situations can help you deal with anger issues before they start. If running late for appointments or rushing your children out the door to school always irritates you, look for creative ways around these situations. Give yourself an extra hour to get ready for an appointment; do some advance planning the night before so you have less to do during the morning rush.

If driving in slow traffic edges your blood pressure to the boiling point, pull off the road. Stop and watch clouds for five minutes. Take another route. Show your children by your example that you can deal with anger in healthy ways that won't hurt others. In irritating, frustrating, or urgent situations, you and your children can stop, think, and choose an alternative to getting angry.

God's Word encourages moms and children to live in peace. But God knows there will be times when you will get irritated, frustrated, or even angry with your children. In those times remember that no one has the right to take out his or her anger on someone else. Let yourself cool down before you speak or act. Take a walk; go into another room; close your eyes and count to ten—just don't walk away from the problem forever. God wants you to deal with the situation, to resolve your anger issues. Ephesians 4:26 encourages moms to resolve angry moments before sunset so that anger won't have time to grow into resentment.

Look closely at anger in your home. If it's caused by an injustice, see if you can correct it. One child may feel another has received undue attention. He or she may feel betrayed by a friend. Seek to correct those problems, too, as you defuse the anger. If you yourself are the source of someone's anger, be quick with an apology. Even if you feel the anger is misplaced, Proverbs 15:1 says that a defensive posture will only aggravate the situation, so apologize. Your children will see your willingness to ask for forgiveness and will learn to follow the same principle in their own lives. Finally, when you or your children refuse to respond to a situation in anger, give yourselves a pat on the back. By not acting hastily in response to anger, you can help set a firm foundation for a peaceful home.

I Will

Be more aware of the situations that can turn my
frustration and irritation into anger.

yes   *no*

Acknowledge that no one has the right to take out
anger on anyone else.

yes   *no*

Remember to flood the fires of anger with the
peacefulness of prayer.

yes   *no*

Concede that my children look to me as their example
on how to handle anger.

yes   *no*

Trust God to show me constructive ways to deal with
my children's and my anger.

yes   *no*

Things to Do

☐ *Whisper in your child's ear during an angry outburst. The unexpected action could create giggles.*

☐ *If a child throws an angry tantrum, leave the room. No audience, no more outbursts.*

☐ *Short-circuit anger by calling for a short time-out or rest time.*

☐ *To encourage healthy venting of anger, have your children draw pictures of their angry moments.*

☐ *Let your children play an instrument as loudly as they want to defuse their anger.*

☐ *Share an experience with your child that made you angry. Tell how you handled it.*

☐ *When your child is angry, give him or her an extra hug, reassuring the child of your love.*

Things to Remember

Now you yourselves are to put off all these: anger, wrath, malice, blasphemy, filthy language out of your mouth.

COLOSSIANS 3:8 NKJV

Dear friends: Lead with your ears, follow up with your tongue, and let anger straggle along in the rear. God's righteousness doesn't grow from human anger.

JAMES 1:19–20 THE MESSAGE

Patience is better than strength. Controlling your temper is better than capturing a city.
Proverbs 16:32 NCV

Those who control their anger have great understanding; those with a hasty temper will make mistakes.

PROVERBS 14:29 NLT

An angry person causes trouble; a person with a quick temper sins a lot.

PROVERBS 29:22 NCV

Do not be a friend of one who has a bad temper, and never keep company with a hothead, or you will learn his ways and set a trap for yourself.

PROVERBS 22:24–25 GOD'S WORD

When you are angry, do not sin, and be sure to stop being angry before the end of the day.

 EPHESIANS 4:26 NCV

A gentle answer will calm a person's anger, but an unkind answer will cause more anger.

PROVERBS 15:1 NCV

Do not hasten in your spirit to be angry, for anger rests in the bosom of fools.

ECCLESIASTES 7:9 KJV

If you are angry with a brother or sister, you will be judged. If you say bad things to a brother or sister, you will be judged by the council.

MATTHEW 5:22 NCV

The LORD shows mercy and is kind. He does not become angry quickly, and he has great love.

PSALM 103:8 NCV

You cannot stay angry with your people forever, because you delight in showing mercy.

MICAH 7:18 NLT

How much more grievous are the consequences of anger than the causes of it.

—MARCUS AURELIUS

A want of patience, a want of kindness, a want of generosity, a want of courtesy, a want of unselfishness, are all instantaneously symbolized in one flash of Temper.

HENRY DRUMMOND

Encouragement

A Powerful Motivator

Encourage one another and build each other up.

—1 THESSALONIANS 5:11 NIV

Picture a crisp autumn evening with two football teams benched on either side of a school gridiron. What would happen to those teams if the stadium stayed empty during their game? They probably wouldn't play very well, would they? They would lack enthusiasm, focus, and energy. The encouragement from cheerleaders, band members, and fans stirs athletes to play their best, because encouragement is a powerful motivator.

You know that from personal experience. When you're tired and grumpy, it's easy to feel discouraged and pessimistic. Yet if someone smiles at you, says a kind word, or offers you a pat on the back, you find yourself bathed in courage with a hope that will get you through the day. Even without those physical cues, moms can find daily encouragement in God's Word. By drawing near to God "with a sincere heart and a sure faith" (Hebrews 10:22 NCV), you can find yourself climbing out from under piles of dirty dishes and laundry with a renewed optimism and cheerful outlook. Spending time in God's presence is a sure way for moms to find encouragement.

Encouragement is contagious, too. When you're feeling chipper, you smile more at others. When you feel confident, you stand taller and treat others with respect. When you are encouraged, you are more apt to think about others and help them "show love and do good deeds" (Hebrews 10:24 NCV).

No one needs encouragement more than your kids. Children face challenges every day, just like adults do. So tell your children often what they are doing right. Offer more praise than criticism. If they need correction for inappropriate behavior, remember to add your encouragement, too, assuring them you know they will do better next time. Be specific and creative in your encouragement.

Whether tots or teens, encouraging your kids in their activities, projects, or in ways they use their own unique talents will build long-term results of good behavior and confidence. Reminding children that they are valuable to God, that God has a significant role for them to play in His kingdom and plan will encourage them in their spiritual lives, too, and give them the strength they need to stay true to their faith.

Encouragement *is* a powerful motivator. Just as encouragement energizes athletes to move down the field to scoring position, so the affirmation and sincere words of praise you give your kids will give them the direction, focus, and energy they need for a good self-image and for passing along encouragement to others, too.

I Will

Spend time with God to find the encouragement
I need.

yes _____ no _____

Find encouragement knowing that I am valuable
to God and His kingdom.

yes _____ no _____

Remind myself that receiving encouragement makes
me a better encourager, too.

yes _____ no _____

Remember that encouragement brings direction,
focus, and energy to my days.

yes _____ no _____

Seek to make sharing encouragement a daily habit.

yes _____ no _____

Picture myself as my children's cheerleader,
encouraging them to the goal of a godly life.

yes _____ no _____

Things to Do

☐ *Read Mark 6:45–51 with your kids. Discuss how Jesus encouraged His disciples.*

☐ *List the gifts God has given your children. Find new ways to encourage their use.*

☐ *Write a letter to each child expressing praise for something he or she does well.*

☐ *Pray together for God to show your kids ways to encourage others at school.*

☐ *Schedule time with your children to encourage them in a new activity, project, or talent.*

☐ *Play an encouragement game. See which child gives the most compliments before the day's over.*

Things to Remember

I know the thoughts that I think toward you, says the LORD, thoughts of peace and not of evil, to give you a future and a hope.

JEREMIAH 29:11 NKJV

May our Lord Jesus Christ himself and God our Father encourage you and strengthen you in every good thing you do and say.

2 THESSALONIANS 2:16 NCV

Now may the God who gives perseverance and encouragement grant you to be of the same mind with one another according to Christ Jesus.

ROMANS 15:5 NASB

God loved us, and through his grace he gave us a good hope and encouragement that continues forever.

2 THESSALONIANS 2:17 NCV

The LORD is my strength and song, and He has become my salvation; He is my God, and I will praise Him.

EXODUS 15:2 NKJV

When I fall, I will arise; when I sit in darkness, the LORD will be a light to me.

MICAH 7:8 NKJV

Correction does much, but encouragement does more. Encouragement after censure is as the sun after a shower.

—JOHANN WOLFGANG VON GOETHE

Encouragement is one of God's most joyous art forms . . . Some people combine a helping hand with a word of praise and produce a grateful heart.

—SUSAN LENZKES

Responsibility

Count on It

Whatever a man sows, that he will also reap.

—GALATIANS 6:7 NKJV

Did you know that King David learned much of the dependability he exhibited in later years as a young person on the family ranch? When Samuel first visited David's home, he found the young teen caring for the family's sheep all by himself. David was too young for military service like his brothers, but he was totally responsible for the family's flock—and did the job well, too. Research indicates that the longer you delay in assigning a child responsibilities, the harder it will be for your child to learn the basics of reliability and dependability later on. So, help your kids learn to be responsible now for . . .

Some household chores. Though it might be easier to do household chores by yourself instead of having to explain them, demonstrate them, and probably redo parts of them later on, moms weren't put on earth to be the family's maid. Kids can be dependable helpers at home. Because kids want to stay busy, use that desire to your advantage.

Young toddlers can be counted on to get the paper every day, to unpack a few groceries, put toys away, and clean the bottom of a closet. Preschoolers can empty smaller wastebaskets, mop up their own spills, and begin to help vacuum, sweep, and dust. By the time kids reach kindergarten they should be able to set and clear the table, pour their own drinks, and rake the yard. Age appropriate chores help build a child's coordination and a healthy attitude toward work and responsibility, too.

The family pets. Pets instill a sense of responsibility and gentleness in kids. Let your child look after wild animals by keeping the birdbath clean and filled and birdseed stocked in the bird feeder. Assign your child the responsibility to maintain an indoor pet's food and water, cage or sleeping place, and to clean up after the pet if there are accidents. Even a five-year-old can clean out a fish tank and feel the sense of accomplishment in doing a good job. Though pets may mean extra work for you or your kids, your child can be healthier if you have a pet. Doctors believe that childhood allergies will diminish more quickly if kids have regular contact with furry pets.

Daily dependence on a child to help with day-to-day duties of family life will teach lessons of responsibility and trustworthiness. You can count on it—and your kids, too.

I Will

Remind myself that I am not my family's maid.

yes____ no____

Recognize that waiting to assign responsibilities only delays my child's growth and development.

yes____ no____

Remember that my kids can be dependable helpers at home.

yes____ no____

Seek God for ways to help my kids learn to be more responsible.

yes____ no____

Understand that my kids can learn valuable lessons by being held responsible for things.

yes____ no____

Consider that the benefits of sharing responsibilities outweigh the inconveniences.

yes____ no____

Things to Do

- [ ] *Build and hang a birdfeeder with your kids. Assign a child the responsibility to keep it filled.*

- [ ] *Ask each family member to be responsible to find a new recipe to try each month.*

- [ ] *Discuss the responsibilities involved in different political positions: president, governor, mayor.*

- [ ] *To cut your grocery shopping time, give each child the responsibility to find a specific item.*

- [ ] *Assign responsibilities for planning a family vacation. Let one child investigate housing, another meals, and so forth.*

- [ ] *Let your child be responsible to pray one day a week at mealtime.*

Things to Remember

Doing right brings freedom to honest people, but those who are not trustworthy will be caught by their own desires.

PROVERBS 11:6 NCV

An undependable messenger gets into trouble, but a dependable envoy brings healing.

PROVERBS 13:17 GOD'S WORD

The One who called you is completely dependable. If he said it, he'll do it!

1 THESSALONIANS 5:24 THE MESSAGE

Don't try to avoid responsibility by saying you didn't know about it. For God knows all hearts, and he sees you. He keeps watch over your soul.

PROVERBS 24:12 NLT

If God has given you leadership ability, take the responsibility seriously. And if you have a gift for showing kindness to others, do it gladly.

ROMANS 12:8 NLT

People with good understanding will be well liked, but the lives of those who are not trustworthy are hard.

PROVERBS 13:15 NCV

> Do right, and God's recompense to you will be the power to do more right.
> —FREDERICK WILLIAM ROBERTSON

> He who is faithful over a few things is a lord of cities. It does not matter whether you preach in Westminster Abbey, or teach a ragged class, so you be faithful. The faithfulness is all.
> —GEORGE MACDONALD

Gossip

Hurtful Hearsay

Gossip separates the best of friends. —Proverbs 16:28 NLT

Hearsay. Chitchat. Scuttlebutt. Tattling. Rumors. Call it what you will, but whenever one person talks to a second person about a third person, you've got gossip. Gossip fills the magazine racks at supermarkets, permeates the airwaves during political campaigns, and floods phone lines all day long. But God doesn't like gossip. God's Word says that He hates "a witness who lies, and someone who starts arguments among families" (Proverbs 6:19 NCV). These traits are the pieces of gossip; and these are the things that anger God.

It's a hard task, but moms and kids can make their homes gossip free. Start by refusing to say anything bad or embarrassing about family members or friends. One grandmother confided to a roomful of new moms that she had promised God when she was a young bride to never say anything negative about her husband to anyone else, even her kids. Such comments would have undermined her kids' respect for their father.

Another mom admitted she often slipped into gossip without meaning to, but had asked God to help her say only good things about her friends, family, or neighbors. If you do hear negative gossip, God's Word suggests you can change its outcome. Whenever you hear something negative about someone else, counter that information immediately with something good.

Another way to stop gossip is to keep it from being repeated, for "where there is no talebearer, the strife ceaseth" (Proverbs 26:20 KJV). This is a tough lesson for kids to learn. What mom hasn't had a child come and tattle about the actions of another one. If gossip is one person talking to a second person about a third person, any child who comes to you tattling about another sibling is opening the door to gossip. While the other child's deeds *might* require parental intervention, experienced moms stop a tattler in mid-sentence, refusing the talebearer an opportunity to speak until all parties are together in the same room. In this way all sides of a problem come to light, including who or what started it, why it's continuing, and whether or not it's dangerous, destructive, or expensive. By wrapping the problem's information with prayer, a mom can more easily find the wisdom of Solomon and a workable solution to the problem.

So leave the hurtful hearsay, chitchat, scuttlebutt, tattling, and rumors to sleazy magazines and faceless politicians. Words can hurt. But words can heal and build up, too, especially when you refuse to start, pass along, or partake in gossip.

I Will

Keep in mind that words have the power to hurt or heal.

yes _____ no _____

Understand that God is displeased with gossip.

yes _____ no _____

Be sensitive to the ways that my gossiping can hurt others.

yes _____ no _____

Realize that listening to gossip is as wrong as passing it on.

yes _____ no _____

Actively look for ways to turn negative gossip around into something good.

yes _____ no _____

Ask God to help me make my home and family gossip free.

yes _____ no _____

Things to Do

☐ *Remember the times someone has gossiped about you. Ask God to help you forgive and forget.*

☐ *Devise a response your kids can use when someone gossips: change the subject, leave the room, and so on.*

☐ *Compose and sign a family contract stating your intent to refuse to listen to gossip.*

☐ *Require tattlers to try and solve problems with siblings before coming to you.*

☐ *Ask your kids to share their experiences with gossip. Gain their commitment to stop gossiping.*

☐ *Journal your thoughts on the ways gossip has adversely affected your family or friends.*

Things to Remember

When you run out of wood, the fire goes out; when the gossip ends, the quarrel dies down.

PROVERBS 26:20 THE MESSAGE

Whoever goes around as a gossip tells secrets. Do not associate with a person whose mouth is always open.

PROVERBS 20:19 GOD'S WORD

Whoever forgives someone's sin makes a friend, but gossiping about the sin breaks up friendships.

PROVERBS 17:9 NCV

Those who are careful about what they say keep themselves out of trouble.

PROVERBS 21:23 NCV

There is one who speaks like the piercings of a sword, but the tongue of the wise promotes health.

PROVERBS 12:18 NKJV

Let everything you say be good and helpful, so that your words will be an encouragement to those who hear them.

EPHESIANS 4:29 NLT

He who hunts for flowers will find flowers; and he who loves weeds will find weeds.

—HENRY WARD BEECHER

I have no regard for truth, no respect for justice . . . My victims are as numerous as the sands of the sea . . . I never forget and seldom forgive. My name is Gossip.

—MORGAN BLAKE

Rest

Seventy Days

Rest in the LORD, and wait patiently for Him.

—PSALM 37:7 NKJV

Jesus understood the pressure of a full schedule. Many people came to Him for physical healing. Others, like Nicodemus, sought Jesus' advice on spiritual problems. God's Word says that the same day Jesus healed Simon Peter's mother, the whole town gathered at Peter's door seeking healing and comfort, too. Jesus ministered into the night to care for each one. Yet Jesus was able to handle demanding days like this because He "departed to a solitary place; and there He prayed" (Mark 1:35 KJV). Solitude, prayer, and rest gave Jesus the refreshment He needed to continue His active ministry.

Moms need the refreshment found in rest, too. Research indicates that stress multiplies when tragedies like death, divorce, unemployment, or major illness occur. Yet moms also experience stress when small problems pile up, one on top of the other—the dog runs away; the baby cries with colic; the boss needs that report today; the vacuum cleaner blows up; the kids need transportation to school, games, appointments, and lessons. The constant pressure of being a mom is tiring, and trying to conquer such endless stress is wearing.

Yet many moms find it difficult to rest because God's Word speaks negatively about idleness, describing it as laziness. Moms don't want to be considered lazy, so no matter how tired they are, they keep going and doing. If that has been your pattern, consider this. Though God doesn't want you to be lazy, He doesn't want you to kill yourself with overwork, either. You need rest to hold body and soul together. God knew that when He created you. In fact God insisted that the ancient Israelites observe more than seventy days a year in which "no customary work" was to be done. Overwork kills, but rest refreshes. So choose to handle your active life like Jesus did—get some rest. Here's how.

Get away. An essential part of resting involves physically removing yourself from stressful situations. Hand your little ones over to Dad or a neighbor for a while, and take a walk around the block. Grab a cup of coffee, ignore the chores, and sit in a quiet corner where you can look out the window. Cry your eyes out at the movies. (This is a two-for-one getaway because you get rest at the movies, and your tears are a great stress reliever, too.) Walk the mall for an hour. Bask in the sunshine on the front stoop for a few moments while you drink in some fresh air. Work out at a gym for half an hour. Leave the kids at Grandma's and book yourself into a motel for a night—with or without your husband or dog.

Find rest in God. Mark 1:35 says Jesus slipped away before sunrise to pray in a quiet place. Jesus knew that you can relax and rest when you acknowledge your dependence on God and submit to His leadership. Sit in the late night or early morning stillness of your home—that time between when the kids fall asleep and the delayed-start dishwasher kicks in. Don't fill the silence with words, music, or noise of any kind. Take a deep breath. Find rest in being alone with God. He has promised to help shoulder your load, to take on the yoke of your problems; and a shared load is a lot easier to carry.

Have some fun. Rest makes you better equipped to handle the needs of others, so find some rest from stress through play. Go to a park with your kids—slide down the slide; swing on the swings; play in the sandbox; whoop and holler and laugh. Have fun with your food—make chocolate chip pancakes; put squiggly jelly worms on toast; serve milk in canning jars; put catsup faces on your hamburger. Make hats from the weirdest stuff you can find in the house. You already know how to work hard. Now play hard; find rest in fun and laughter.

Genesis 2:2 says that after God created, God rested. If God can balance hard work with intense rest, you can, too. God's Word says you've got seventy days of rest available. Why not take *one* day's rest from stress today?

I Will

Know that I am a valuable person to God. ___*yes*___ ___*no*___

Appreciate the skills and strength God has given me for mothering my kids. ___*yes*___ ___*no*___

Recognize that constant stress is not what God has in His plan for me. ___*yes*___ ___*no*___

Admit that when I'm stressed I'm often not at my best. ___*yes*___ ___*no*___

Remind myself that God wants me to find time to rest from stress. ___*yes*___ ___*no*___

Things to Do

☐ *Before you go to sleep thank God for the fun people in your life.*

☐ *With your littlest kids, dress up like clowns and walk the mall to relieve stress.*

☐ *Pray with a friend who is overworked and overstressed.*

☐ *Organize a mom's night out for you and two other overstressed moms to have fun.*

☐ *Make the bathroom off limits to problems so you'll have a quiet place to rest.*

☐ *Schedule a babysitter for two hours of rest from stress time. Do whatever you want.*

☐ *Put the kids to bed. Then soak in a bubble bath and relax with a good book.*

Things to Remember

Come to Me, all you who labor and are heavy laden, and I will give you rest.

MATTHEW 11:28 NKJV

He gives strength to those who are tired and more power to those who are weak.

ISAIAH 40:29 NCV

I will give rest and strength to those who are weak and tired.
Jeremiah 31:25 NCV

It is vain for you to rise up early, to retire late, to eat the bread of painful labors; for He gives to His beloved even in his sleep.

PSALM 127:2 NASB

He said, "My Presence will go with you, and I will give you rest."

EXODUS 33:14 NKJV

He who dwells in the shelter of the Most High will rest in the shadow of the Almighty.

PSALM 91:1 NIV

He makes me to lie down in green pastures; He leads me beside the still waters. He restores my soul.

PSALM 23:2–3 NKJV

He said to them, "Come aside by yourselves to a deserted place and rest a while." For there were many coming and going, and they did not even have time to eat.

MARK 6:31 NKJV

O God, You are more awesome than Your holy places. The God of Israel is He who gives strength and power to His people. Blessed be God!

PSALM 68:35 NKJV

Therefore, a time of rest and worship exists for God's people. Those who entered his place of rest also rested from their work as God did from his.

HEBREWS 4:9–10 GOD'S WORD

Let the beloved of the LORD rest secure in him, for he shields him all day long, and the one the LORD loves rests between his shoulders.

DEUTERONOMY 33:12 NIV

Blessed be the Lord, who daily loads us with benefits, the God of our salvation!

PSALM 68:19 NKJV

God . . . authorizes us to take that rest and refreshment which are necessary to keeping up the strength of mind and body.

—SAINT JOHN BAPTISTE DE LA SALLE

If we could learn how to balance rest against effort, calmness against strain, quiet against turmoil, we would assure ourselves of joy in living.

—JOSEPHINE RATHBONE

Grandparents

From Troublesome to Terrific

Old people are proud of their grandchildren, and children are proud of their parents.   —PROVERBS 17:6 NCV

Grandparents are one of your child's greatest assets. Sharing stories from your childhood that might embarrass you but definitely delight your children, grandparents form a vital link between your child and your heritage, culture, values, and character. Listening to stories about you, catching a glimpse of themselves reflected in grandma's eyes or grandpa's hairline, your children will find a true sense of connection to family.

Yet grandparents, without meaning to, can sometimes be troublesome to moms. Grandparents can undermine discipline and diet, spoiling their grandchildren with too many treats or stepping in to lessen the blow of a punishment. Grandparents have a knack for taking over at times and for being overly generous in reminding you, mom, of your own faults when you were that age, too.

However, you can set the tone for a good relationship with the grandparents in your family. If you fall apart every time your child gets sick, gets in a fight, or brings home straight D's on a report card, grandparents are likely to step in and tell you how to raise the grandchildren. On the contrary, if you act competent in dealing with your children, grandparents won't try to take over. Yes, they'll have ideas and opinions. But letting grandparents know in advance that you love them and want them involved in your kids' lives, that you'll ask for help if you ever need it, and that you'll call if you have problems, will be the reassurance grandparents need to chew their fingernails in silence.

Be considerate of the grandparents in your life, too. Some grandparents can't wait to babysit their grandkids. Others might be afraid to take on that responsibility. Some grandparents might have busy work schedules; some prefer to be left alone most of the time. Whatever your situation, keep reaching out to grandparents and involve them as much as possible in your child's life even through major family changes like divorce or death of a spouse. Keep out-of-town grandparents informed through letters, phone calls, home movies, taped messages, or computer-video link ups. Don't let grandparents miss a milestone. Learning about first steps and potty training is as important to grandparents as it is to moms. Knowing about boyfriends and driver's ed classes will keep grandparents connected to older grandkids, too.

God's Word says grandparents are proud of their grandchildren. With a little help from you, your children's grandparents can also be actively involved in your children's lives, spoiling them with love and attention and receiving the same in return.

I Will

Recognize that grandparents and grandchildren need to get to know one another.

_____ yes _____ no

Understand that some of the things my children learn from their grandparents might be embarrassing.

_____ yes _____ no

Thank God for the rich heritage, culture, values, and history grandparents convey to my children.

_____ yes _____ no

Admit that my children sometimes act like their grandparents as much as look like them.

_____ yes _____ no

Concede that I can set a positive tone for involving grandparents in my children's lives.

_____ yes _____ no

Things to Do

☐ Ask grandparents to audiotape or videotape their memories of earlier times.

☐ Send some artwork or a tracing of your child's hand to each grandparent.

☐ Let your children dictate letters to their grandparents.

☐ Ask a grandparent for a favorite family recipe. Make a copy for each child.

☐ Videotape a grandparent's visit. Let your children watch the tape whenever they want.

☐ Photograph your child throughout a typical week. Make copies of the photos for each grandparent.

Things to Remember

I will be your God throughout your lifetime—until your hair is white with age. I made you, and I will care for you.

ISAIAH 46:4 NLT

The glory of young men is their strength, and the splendor of old men is their gray head.

PROVERBS 20:29 NKJV

The silver-haired head is a crown of glory, if it is found in the way of righteousness.

PROVERBS 16:31 NKJV

Wisdom is with the ancient one. The one who has had many days has insight.

JOB 12:12 GOD'S WORD

We will not hide these truths from our children but will tell the next generation about the glorious deeds of the LORD.

PSALM 78:4 NLT

May the LORD bless you from Zion all the days of your life; may you see the prosperity of Jerusalem, and may you live to see your children's children.

PSALM 128:5–6 NIV

Isn't God good? Generation after generation he provides a fresh set of grandparents, an ever-present counterculture in our busy world.
—CHARLES R. SWINDOLL

If our kids knew what raising kids was really like, we'd never have any grandchildren.
—STAN AND JAN BERENSTAIN

Self-esteem

God's Flowers

We are His workmanship, created in Christ Jesus for good works. —EPHESIANS 2:10 KJV

A springtime flowerbed is a beautiful sight. Tulips intermingle their own unique shape and fragrance with hyacinths, daffodils, and crocuses. These springtime flowers need a good root system, too, to support their beautiful blooms. Gardeners make sure each bulb receives sufficient sunlight, water, and good soil to nourish the roots and help the flower blossom beautifully.

Your children are a lot like flowers, too—the beautiful blooms in God's garden. You are His gardener, providing the sunlight of love, the water of acceptance, and the good soil of instruction to help God's flowers bloom. Like flowers, your kids have a root system, too—their self-esteem. Though kids may have different personalities or limitations, every child needs a nourished self-esteem to become the best bloom in God's garden that he or she can be. You can help your kids achieve a strong, secure sense of self by helping them discover their talents and abilities, treating them with respect and courtesy, and reassuring them that being different from others is okay. Differences merely make each child unique, just as God intended him or her to be.

Your words affect your child's self-esteem, too. The Israelites took this idea to heart when they named their children. Every Jewish name had a meaning—*Emmanuel* meant "God is with us," and *Barnabas* meant "son of encouragement," for instance. When an Israelite mom called her kids in for supper, she was actually reminding herself and her kids what she wanted those kids to be—the grace of God *(Jesse)*, the gift of God *(Matthew)*, a princess *(Sarah)*. In like fashion, whatever you want your children to be—trustworthy, successful, honest, loving—praise your kids for becoming these things. Call to their attention their successes, praise their honesty, thank them for fulfilling a promise, reward their love with more of yours. Give your kids a nickname that embodies uplifting traits, too (smart-stuff, big man, sweet cheeks), instead of labeling them with a negative, though maybe accurate, moniker (needle-nose, four-eyes, slowpoke).

Remember that belittling a child or punishing him in public can tear down a child's self-image. If kids need to be corrected, help them save face by disciplining them in private. Soften your correction with compliments before and after it, always noting that the actions are the "bad" thing, not the child. To further strengthen a child's self-esteem, verbalize at least one affirming statement to each child each day. Your kids will blossom beautifully if you actively care for their root system of self-esteem.

I Will

Accept my kids and myself just as we are, as
beautiful flowers in God's garden.

_____yes_____   _____no_____

Understand that each child will have different
self-esteem needs.

_____yes_____   _____no_____

Realize that I can help my child build a secure,
solid sense of self-esteem.

_____yes_____   _____no_____

Remember that harmful words can tear apart an
individual's sense of self-worth.

_____yes_____   _____no_____

Recognize the value of positive reinforcement
to my child's self-esteem.

_____yes_____   _____no_____

Determine to treat my children with courtesy and
respect to build their self-esteem.

_____yes_____   _____no_____

Things to Do

☐ *Research the meaning of your child's name to find the self-esteem
message hidden within it.*

☐ *Draw self-portraits with your kids to highlight any self-esteem problems
you may need to resolve.*

☐ *Write thank-you notes to people who have boosted your child's self-
esteem in some way.*

☐ *Read Charles Boyd's* Different Children Different Needs *to match
different personality types and self-esteem needs.*

☐ *With your kids, write a self-esteem rap that states one or two positive
traits about each other.*

Things to Remember

God is with you; the mighty One will save you. He will rejoice over you. You will rest in his love; he will sing and be joyful about you.

ZEPHANIAH 3:17 NCV

You made [human beings] a little lower than the angels and crowned them with glory and honor. You put them in charge of everything you made.

PSALM 8:5–6 NCV

I will praise You, for I am fearfully and wonderfully made; marvelous are Your works, and that my soul knows very well.

PSALM 139:14 NKJV

Whoever is a believer in Christ is a new creation. The old way of living has disappeared. A new way of living has come into existence.

2 CORINTHIANS 5:17 GOD'S WORD

Put on the new self, which in the likeness of God has been created in righteousness and holiness of the truth.

EPHESIANS 4:24 NASB

Look at the birds of the air, for they neither sow nor reap nor gather into barns; yet your heavenly Father feeds them. Are you not of more value than they?

MATTHEW 6:26 NKJV

If you really do put a small value upon yourself, rest assured that the world will not raise your price.

—AUTHOR UNKNOWN

An important part of raising a child is to literally raise their self-worth, their sights, and their faith. That kind of raising is the product of praising.

—AUTHOR UNKNOWN

Thanksgiving

An Endless Attitude

In everything give thanks; for this is the will of God in Christ Jesus concerning you. —1 THESSALONIANS 5:18 KJV

Friends and family gather together on the fourth Thursday of November to scrutinize parades, armchair quarterback the football games, and do deadly damage to large turkeys, spiral-sliced hams, and pumpkin pies. As you blow out the Pilgrim-shaped candles, zip leftovers into plastic bags for Grandma to take home, and put the washed-and-dried platters back into the cupboard, you might actually look around and breathe a prayer of gratitude that you survived another Thanksgiving. But giving thanks doesn't have to begin and end on a Thursday in November. True thanksgiving can be a yearlong attitude of the heart.

True thanksgiving brings life into a different focus. The apostle Paul urged Christians to give thanks for everything. That includes the hard things in life, too. It's easy to be thankful for good things, but how can you be thankful for illness, injury, or pain? Look at it this way: If you examine a tapestry you'll see dark and light threads. The weaver who planned the beautiful design knew the dark threads were needed to set off the lighter colored threads of gold and silver.

If you think of God as a master weaver who is making your life into a beautiful tapestry, you can view the hard things of life from a different angle, from God's perspective. God has a good plan for your life. Knowing that He has promised to take the sad and make it into something glad can make your heart thankful whether you're facing good days or bad ones.

Thankfulness can affect the way you pray, too. Prayers for God's help often reflect the I-need, I-want, or please-do-this attitude. A heart that always gives thanks begins prayers with, "Thank you, God." Instead of praying, "Help my husband find a job, and show us how to make ends meet," a grateful heart could pray, "Thank you, God, for providing a job for my husband; thanks for showing us how to stretch our finances, too" even if there's no job offer on the horizon. Thanking God in advance keeps you focused on Him and voices your faith in His power to answer prayer, too.

But thankfulness is also a *giving* thing. God's Word says that when you "give," God blesses. Though God wants you to be generous with your things, that's only one facet to giving. God generously blesses you for extravagant *thanks*-giving, too. Think about it. When your heart is thankful, you are usually more encouraged, more positive, more happy. What wonderful blessings. When your heart is thankful, your kids benefit, too. A happy, positive, encouraged mom is a better example, a better teacher, a better friend. A thankful heart is also a healthier heart. Medical researchers know that an attitude of gratefulness can reduce stress levels, blood pressure, and aches and pains. An attitude of gratitude is a pretty good thing.

To cultivate thanksgiving in your family's daily life and help your children learn a "Thank you, God" attitude in prayer, set aside one day a week for thankful prayers only. You can expand your thankful heart attitudes around the house, too. Tuck a note of appreciation into a lunchbox or backpack. Give an unexpected hug and thank you to children who are only half finished with their chores. Include others in your thanksgiving, too. Whenever you receive a gift (at Christmas, birthdays, special occasions) acknowledge each gift with a thank-you note. If you can, include a photo of the gift being used.

You can also send notes to folks who rarely get thanked for the work they do—the crossing guard who protects your children on their way to school; the friendly checkout person at the grocery store; the mailman or delivery person who takes care of your packages. You might want to send a letter to the editor of your paper, thanking a city official or other public servant for the job he or she does for you and your community. Look around—there are many folks to whom you and your children could say thanks.

Yes, thanksgiving is more than pumpkin pie and Pilgrims; more than family and friends, feasting and fun. Thanksgiving is more than a holiday. It's an endless attitude of gratitude. Do you have it?

I Will

Thank God for the privilege of living in a country that celebrates thankfulness.

_____ yes _____ no

Linger over memories of past Thanksgiving holidays, truly giving thanks for family.

_____ yes _____ no

Focus my heart on the blessings God has given for which I can be thankful.

_____ yes _____ no

Trust God to bring good out of bad situations and circumstances.

_____ yes _____ no

Put my thanks before my requests when I come to God in prayer.

_____ yes _____ no

Remember that maintaining a thankful heart makes me a healthier, happier mom.

_____ yes _____ no

Things to Do

☐ *Write a note to a relative, sharing some reasons why you're thankful for them.*

☐ *Whenever you see a rainbow, list five things about your children you are thankful for.*

☐ *Compose a family prayer of thanksgiving. Say it at bedtime for a whole week.*

☐ *Label paper chain links with things you're thankful for. Decorate a bedroom with the chain.*

☐ *Invite a stranger to share in a thanksgiving dinner, even if it isn't November.*

☐ *Buy something special to say thank you: stickers for a teacher or flowers for Grandma.*

Things to Remember

As you therefore have received Christ Jesus the Lord, so walk in Him, rooted and built up in Him and established in the faith, as you have been taught, abounding in it with thanksgiving.

COLOSSIANS 2:6–7 NKJV

Thanks be to God, who always leads us in victory through Christ. God uses us to spread his knowledge everywhere like a sweet-smelling perfume.

2 CORINTHIANS 2:14 NCV

Everything God created is good,
and nothing is to be rejected if it
is received with thanksgiving.
1 Timothy 4:4 NIV

Let them give thanks to the LORD for his love and for the miracles he does for people.

PSALM 107:21 NCV

Thanks be to God, who gives us the victory through our Lord Jesus Christ.

1 CORINTHIANS 15:57 NKJV

I will give thanks to the LORD because of his righteousness and will sing praise to the name of the LORD Most High.

PSALM 7:17 NIV

Enter into His gates with thanksgiving, and into His courts with praise. Be thankful to Him, and bless His name.

PSALM 100:4 NKJV

Oh, give thanks to the LORD, for He is good! For His mercy endures forever. Let the redeemed of the LORD say so.

PSALM 107:1–2 NKJV

Oh come, let us sing to the LORD! Let us shout joyfully to the Rock of our salvation. Let us come before His presence with thanksgiving.

PSALM 95:1–2 NKJV

I'm about to burst with song; I can't keep quiet about you. GOD, my God, I can't thank you enough.

PSALM 30:12 THE MESSAGE

Oh give thanks to the LORD, call upon His name; make known His deeds among the peoples.

1 CHRONICLES 16:8 NASB

I will offer to You the sacrifice of thanksgiving, and will call upon the name of the LORD.

PSALM 116:17 NKJV

When we learn to give thanks, we are learning to concentrate not on the bad things, but on the good things in our lives.

—AMY VANDERBILT

Two kinds of gratitude: The sudden kind we feel for what we take; the larger kind we feel for what we give.

—EDWIN ARLINGTON ROBINSON

Sharing with Others

Learning to Let Go

Do not forget to do good to others, and share with them, because such sacrifices please God. —HEBREWS 13:16 NCV

One of the first things a baby learns is to grasp something and hold on. One baby girl learned this lesson so well she grabbed her hair and then cried in pain, quizzically looking at her mother, wondering who was pulling her hair. This tiny tot had mastered the art of grasping and holding, but she needed to learn another lesson, too. She needed to learn to let go.

Learning to let go means losing your hold on something. Children can resent a new baby or a visitor in the house because it means a loss of importance, status, or power. Yet letting go plays a big part in sharing and helping others. God's Word reminds moms "to be rich in doing good deeds, to be generous and ready to share" (1 Timothy 6:18 NCV). Though sharing goes against early lessons of holding on, letting go is essential to helping others.

Children won't truly grasp the concept of sharing until they are three or four years old, but you can begin to teach sharing at eighteen months. Help your children share their toys by regulating turns with favorite toys with a timer. To demonstrate fairness in sharing, let a three-year-old break a cookie or treat in half; let your other child choose the piece he or she wants. To learn the blessings of generosity, help your children sort through their outgrown clothes and find outfits to share with less fortunate kids. To train your kids to look beyond their own needs, let your toddler welcome a new neighbor with a bouquet of dandelions, a preschooler help you deliver a meal to a sick friend, or your teen assist you with a chore or errand for an elderly family member.

Your children will also learn to help others if you show them that sharing is an expression of love. Encourage your children to make homemade gifts for Christmas. The work a child does for others, whether in the kitchen, workshop, or garden, is a practical way to demonstrate love. Make volunteering meaningful, too. Your local animal shelter needs dog walkers. Your church may know some older adults who need their grass cut or leaves raked. Habitat for Humanity needs teen volunteers to help build homes for the needy. Meals on Wheels may need kitchen or packaging help.

Holding on comes easily to everyone. Letting go and sharing with others is tougher, but God's Word says sharing will yield a spiritual reward: "such sacrifices please God" (Hebrews 13:16 NCV).

I Will

Acknowledge that sharing can be hard to learn, but necessary for helping others. _yes_ _no_

Be willing to be an example to my children of sharing and helping others. _yes_ _no_

Ask God to show my children and me opportunities to serve others. _yes_ _no_

Know that God is pleased when my family and I share and help others. _yes_ _no_

Understand that learning to share will yield positive results in my children's lives. _yes_ _no_

Remember that serving and sharing are practical ways of showing my love. _yes_ _no_

Things to Do

☐ *Make time to help out in a homeless shelter or soup kitchen.*

☐ *Check with your school or church youth group about volunteer service programs.*

☐ *Offer to tutor an adult who wants to learn to read. Let your children help.*

☐ *Babysit a friend's child to give her a break.*

☐ *Visit an older relative. Ask each child to bring or say something nice.*

☐ *Make handmade thinking-of-you cards to send to older adults in convalescent homes.*

☐ *Let your children choose three of their toys to share with homeless or hospitalized children.*

Things to Remember

Whoever desires to become great among you, let him be your servant. And whoever desires to be first among you, let him be your slave—just as the Son of Man did not come to be served, but to serve.

MATTHEW 20:26–28 NKJV

Do not look out only for yourselves. Look out for the good of others also.

1 CORINTHIANS 10:24 NCV

Strength is for service, not status. Each one of us needs to look after the good of the people around us, asking ourselves, "How can I help?"

ROMANS 15:1–2 THE MESSAGE

The greatest among you will be your servant. For whoever exalts himself will be humbled, and whoever humbles himself will be exalted.

MATTHEW 23:11–12 NIV

Command them to do good, to be rich in good deeds, and to be generous and willing to share.

1 TIMOTHY 6:18 NIV

The King will answer and say to them, "Assuredly, I say to you, inasmuch as you did it to one of the least of these My brethren, you did it to Me."

MATTHEW 25:40 NKJV

We should do a service to a friend to build him closer; to an enemy, to make a friend of him.

—CLEOBULUS

The world cannot always understand one's profession of faith, but it can understand service.

—IAN MACLAREN

Hospitality

Forget the Feast

Share with God's people who are in need. Practice hospitality. —ROMANS 12:13 NIV

What comes to mind when you think of hospitality? Lavish themed dinner parties or sipping a cup of tea with a lonely neighbor? A barbeque in the backyard for your church group or an open door to a latchkey kid? Actually all these activities fall under the banner of hospitality—the opening of your home and heart to guests or strangers in a warm, friendly, generous way.

God urged the ancient Israelites to show hospitality to strangers because they knew from experience what it was like to live in the foreign land of Egypt, what it felt like to be alone, left out, and unaccepted. The apostle Paul expanded on this lesson in Romans 15, reminding Christians that before receiving the message of salvation all people were foreigners to God's family. Paul therefore urges all Christians to open their hearts in hospitality to others because God opened His heart to them.

But sharing hospitality with others seems easier said than done. Your to-do list is never empty; there's just no time; you feel like you're neglecting your own kids too much already without adding more to your schedule. You know you're not a gifted hostess like those television moms or funny like Bill Cosby or rich enough to lay out a lavish feast. So what can you do, as Romans 12:13 says, to practice hospitality?

True hospitality starts in the home. Your kids are a precious gift from God, little strangers who come into life with their own unique needs. Give your children what every stranger wants—love, acceptance, friendship, safety. Your kids' friends are your second opportunity for hospitality. Ignore the muddy footprints, scattered toys, and incessant chatter that come when these little visitors invade your home. Remember, instead, that these children are created in God's image, too. Show them the respect and dignity they may not receive in their own homes. Introduce them to God's acceptance and love (when they fight with your kids), grace and forgiveness (when they break something).

Then broaden your horizons. Look around your church, neighborhood, or place of work. Is there a single mom, a lonely widow, or a latchkey kid who wouldn't care about your under-the-bed-dust-bunnies and chipped dishes but would love a cup of cocoa and a smile? Forget the feast that costs a king's ransom. Share what you have with others you while you're doing what you normally do. Share your heart in your home—for that's what true hospitality is all about.

I Will

Understand that people of all ages need to receive acceptance and hospitality.

yes   *no*

Remember what it feels like to be alone, left out, and unaccepted.

yes   *no*

Thank God for those who have reached out in hospitality to my children and me.

yes   *no*

Recognize that God can use me just as I am to show hospitality to others.

yes   *no*

Show hospitality to my family as much as I do to those who visit us.

yes   *no*

Open my heart and find creative, inexpensive ways to make hospitality a lifestyle choice.

yes   *no*

Things to Do

☐ *Draw pictures of angels as a reminder of the hospitality surprise hidden in Hebrews 13:2.*

☐ *With your kids, brainstorm ideas for adding warmth and hospitality to your home.*

☐ *Purchase a teapot as a family reminder to be hospitable. Make tea whenever someone visits.*

☐ *Pray and ask God to make each room in your home a place for hospitality.*

☐ *Decide on an inexpensive, simple meal you can keep on hand for unexpected visitors.*

☐ *Offer to greet strangers at the door of your church before worship service.*

Things to Remember

Do not neglect to show hospitality to strangers, for by this some have entertained angels without knowing it.

HEBREWS 13:2 NASB

Share your food with the hungry and bring poor, homeless people into your own homes. When you see someone who has no clothes, give him yours.

ISAIAH 58:7 NCV

Cheerfully share your home with those who need a meal or a place to stay.

1 PETER 4:9 NLT

Don't hesitate to accept hospitality, because those who work deserve to be fed.

MATTHEW 10:10 NLT

She must be known for her good works—works such as raising her children, welcoming strangers, washing the feet of God's people, helping those in trouble, and giving her life to do all kinds of good deeds.

1 TIMOTHY 5:10 NCV

When you give a feast, invite the poor, the maimed, the lame, the blind. And you will be blessed.

LUKE 14:13–14 NKJV

The crown of the house is godliness; the beauty of the house is order; the glory of the house is hospitality; the blessing of the house is contentment.

—HENRY VAN DYKE

Every heart filled with love is a home for the Savior. Every home filled with love is a witness to the world.

—STEPHANIE MICHELE

Kids and Communication

Tongue Twisters

People will be rewarded for what they say.

Rubber baby buggy bumpers. Can you repeat that tongue twister quickly fifteen times in a row? Speaking clearly and distinctly is important to good communication. Being careful of *what* you say is important, too. God's Word says you will be judged by your words, for "the mouth speaks the things that are in the heart" (Matthew 12:34 NCV). To improve daily communication with your kids and others, begin by improving the attitude of your heart. Connecting with God on a regular basis will fill your heart with His love, kindness, joy, and understanding. With a heart full of those positive traits, there won't be much room left for grouchiness, frustration, or selfishness to grow.

Then consider your kids' communication skills. Teach babies to talk by looking at them and using clear, distinct words with a pleasant tone of voice. (Save the singsong, oochy-coochy baby talk for your pets.) Read aloud to your high-chair kids from the back of the cereal box so they learn to associate all language with communication. As your child learns to communicate, be respectful of each other. You wouldn't want to be in a room with two other people and not be included in the conversation, so show your child the same courtesy. Include your child in conversations you have with others by asking an occasional opinion, if appropriate, or informing your child of your need to converse privately with another person.

Once kids begin to talk, they take every opportunity to do so. To limit conversational interruptions, teach your kids to wait their turn to talk by putting your finger to your lips whenever they interrupt. Help them pay attention to the flow of words, listening for stopping points. Much like cars that stop and go at traffic lights, good communicators go (speak) when others stop, and stop (listen) when others talk. Interruptions should begin with "excuse me, please . . ." to indicate a child's desire to be heard, too.

As your kids' language skills increase they will likely pick up bad words. Unfortunately, they'll hit you with these bad words at the most inappropriate times, too, like the child who chanted a vulgar word repeatedly as he skipped past the pastor following Sunday's sermon. (The boy mistakenly thought the word was the sound of a chicken's cackle.) If your child does voice a vulgar term or curse word, pull that child aside to a quiet place. Let your child know that the word is not a nice word and should never be repeated. The mother of the Sunday chicken-cackling boy merely gave the young man the true sound of the chicken's cry and the boy happily gave up the vulgarity—much to the embarrassed mother's relief.

As verbal skills increase, so does the misuse of words. Lying can become a problem for preschoolers. If you discover a broken lamp and know your toddler and the goldfish were the only ones in the room, you'll have a good idea of the lamp breaker's identity. Yet lies pop out easily in response to yes or no questions or to "Who did that?" Help your child tell the truth by asking how questions instead—"How did the lamp get broken?" If your child tells the truth, reward it openly and lavishly. However, if a lie persists, send the child to a corner with the instruction, "Bend over and touch your toes" or "Spin around twice." Giving your child this save-face activity may help your child find the truth.

Be truthful when you speak with your kids, too, to reinforce the importance of truthful communication. For example, if a child needs a shot at the doctor's office, be honest and say, "This will hurt, but Mommy's right here with you." Don't try to make something appear better than it is, either. That's as bad as lying. Saying "You'll love this" sets everyone up for disappointment. If you speak truth in these things, your children will be able to trust your words about other things, too.

So practice wrapping your tongue around good words, truthful communication, and conversations that respect each other. If the things you think about and the things you say are acceptable in God's sight you might find yourself untwisting your tongue enough to try "She sells seashells down by the seashore."

I Will

	yes	no
Be aware that what I say reflects what's in my heart.		
Look to improve my communication with my kids by improving my connectedness to God.		
Show courtesy and respect in my communication with my kids and others.		
Be careful to correct my child's bad language—and mine, too.		
Be honest in what I say to my kids.		
Remember that my truthful example can encourage my kids to tell the truth, too.		

Things to Do

- [ ] *Playfully practice clear speech. Put mini-marshmallows in your kids' mouths as they say their names.*

- [ ] *To teach kids words are important, watch and discuss the VeggieTales video The Fib from Outer Space.*

- [ ] *To find out what God thinks about your words, do a Bible study about the tongue.*

- [ ] *At each meal today add the nutrient of affirmation to your kids' communication diet.*

- [ ] *Find a library book of tongue twisters. Say them together with your kids to practice clear speech.*

- [ ] *To limit interruptions, provide crayons and newspaper comics for your kids to color during phone calls.*

Things to Remember

Let the words of my mouth and the meditation of my heart be acceptable in Your sight, O LORD, my strength and my Redeemer.

PSALM 19:14 NKJV

Good people bring good things out of the good they stored in their hearts . . . People speak the things that are in their hearts.

LUKE 6:45 NCV

The right word spoken at the right time is as beautiful as gold apples in a silver bowl.
Proverbs 25:11 NCV

The mouths of the righteous utter wisdom, and their tongues speak justice.

PSALM 37:30 NRSV

Speak to each other with psalms, hymns, and spiritual songs, singing and making music in your hearts to the Lord.

EPHESIANS 5:19 NCV

People will be rewarded for what they say; they will be rewarded by how they speak.

PROVERBS 18:20 NCV

Those who are careful about what they say protect their lives, but whoever speaks without thinking will be ruined.

PROVERBS 13:3 NCV

Do any of you want to live a life that is long and good? Then watch your tongue! Keep your lips from telling lies!

PSALM 34:12–13 NLT

Pleasant words are like a honeycomb, sweetness to the soul and health to the bones.

PROVERBS 16:24 NKJV

Let your speech always be with grace, seasoned with salt, that you may know how you ought to answer each one.

COLOSSIANS 4:6 NKJV

We all make many mistakes. If people never said anything wrong, they would be perfect and able to control their entire selves, too.

JAMES 3:2 NCV

Set a guard, O LORD, over my mouth; keep watch over the door of my lips.

PSALM 141:3 NKJV

It is with words as with sunbeams. The more they are condensed, the deeper they burn.

—ROBERT SOUTHEY

A word is not a crystal, transparent and unchanged; it is the skin of a living thought and may vary greatly in color and content according to the circumstances.

—OLIVER WENDELL HOLMES

Sex and Intimacy

We Need to Talk

Make no provision for the flesh, to fulfill its lusts.

—ROMANS 13:14 NKJV

It looked like a typical group of children waiting for the school bus. Then one of the girls turned in profile, displaying the distended abdomen of pregnancy. The sight broke one mother's heart. She began to pray for the child who would soon give birth to another. That evening she said to her children, "We need to talk."

We live in a sex-saturated culture. Sexual programming fills our airwaves. Casual conversations are laced with frequent references to sex. Society has trivialized what God's Word considers sacred. Yet your child's basic attitudes toward sexuality need not reflect music lyrics, sex education classes, or lessons learned in the backseat of a Ford. To help your child remain sexually pure until marriage, you and your children need to talk about sex—honestly, openly, and often. Will you have difficulty doing it? Probably. Will there be moments when your child will nail you with tough questions? Count on it. But you are your child's best teacher about sex.

Mothers and daughters share physical similarities that can help you discuss where babies come from. While teaching your daughter how to shave her legs or about menstruation, you can also talk freely about God's commands against sexual promiscuity. Reassure your daughter it's okay to be a virgin, that there's nothing sexy about giving in to outrageous peer pressure.

Mothers and sons can also share meaningful sexual dialogue. While fathers may deal with sexual mechanics, moms can help sons counteract the pressures of peers and hormones by reminding boys that having sex is not a proof of masculinity. Virginity is not only okay for guys, it's the best choice to make. There will only be one first-time for sex, and that first moment should be shared with a spouse. Remind your child that the sex drive is natural and powerful, but it is also controllable and can be beautiful and fulfilling between two life partners.

Recognize that sexual temptations exist, but there are physical, psychological, and spiritually destructive results to sexual experimentation. Knowing that today's sexually active teens face more than fifty different kinds of sexually transmitted diseases can be a sobering thought for you and your children.

One day your child will face the choice between remaining chaste or giving in to sexual experimentation. Take time now to give your children a godly perspective on sexuality so they can make right decisions about sexual intimacy. Begin your conversation saying, "We need to talk." And then talk honestly, openly, and often about sex.

I Will

Remind myself to pray daily for the sexual purity of
my children and their friends.

_____ yes   _____ no

Refrain from showing shock or embarrassment when
my child asks me about sex.

_____ yes   _____ no

Understand that talking honestly about sex can
help build trust between me and my children.

_____ yes   _____ no

Consider that my attitudes about sex and intimacy
will affect my child's attitudes, too.

_____ yes   _____ no

Accept that others may consider God's sexual
standards unrealistic or overprotective.

_____ yes   _____ no

Things to Do

☐ *Teach small children that only you or a doctor may touch their
private parts.*

☐ *Read and discuss Amy Scheuring's* Sex: More Than a Plumbing Lesson
with your teen.

☐ *Take your teenager with you and volunteer some time at a crisis
pregnancy center.*

☐ *Share with your child how you learned about sex when you were young.*

☐ *To start a sexual dialogue, ask your child's opinion about birth control
or sex before marriage.*

☐ *Remove sexually explicit media and restrict access to sexual websites to
promote purity in your home.*

☐ *Visit www.truelovewaits.com with your teen. Ask him or her to take a
stand for abstinence until marriage.*

Things to Remember

Sexual drives are strong, but marriage is strong enough to contain them and provide for a balanced and fulfilling sexual life in a world of sexual disorder.

1 CORINTHIANS 7:2 THE MESSAGE

Therefore a man shall leave his father and mother and be joined to his wife, and they shall become one flesh.

GENESIS 2:24 NKJV

Let the husband render to his wife the affection due her, and likewise also the wife to her husband.

1 CORINTHIANS 7:3 NKJV

Put to death, therefore, whatever belongs to your earthly nature: sexual immorality, impurity, lust, evil desires and greed, which is idolatry.

COLOSSIANS 3:5 NIV

You are not to associate with anyone who claims to be a Christian yet indulges in sexual sin, or is greedy, or worships idols, or is abusive, or a drunkard, or a swindler. Don't even eat with such people.

1 CORINTHIANS 5:11 NLT

Run away from sexual sin. Every other sin people do is outside their bodies, but those who sin sexually sin against their own bodies.

1 CORINTHIANS 6:18 NCV

The expectation we have of being without bodily appetites in a future life is a very good argument against being under their power in the present life.

—MATTHEW HENRY

Replace sensual thoughts with wholesome ones . . . Scripture memory works wonders, frankly. I find it impossible to simultaneously lust and repeat verses on moral purity.

—CHARLES SWINDOLL

Fun and Laughter

Piano Portraits

Rejoice in the LORD your God's presence.

—DEUTERONOMY 12:18 NCV

You may have seen old-fashioned sepia portraits with dour-looking relatives in black crepe, glaring at an unseen photographer. Even the small children are stony faced. Yet some of these family portraits are different. There's a hint that some of those grim-faced relations might have been fun people to be around.

That perception is probably truer than you realize. Generations ago God's Word was the central focus in family life. Though His Word handles heavy-hitting subjects like faith, surrender, and trust, whole passages of Scripture also deal with happiness, laughter, and joy. These sour-faced sepia relations probably knew how to apply God's words to their lives *and* be fun people in the process. That's what God wants from you, too. Moms are supposed to model God's character to their children, so sharing God's joy, laughter, and happiness in your home can be a fun part of mothering.

Researchers claim that three minutes of belly laughter exercises tummy muscles as much as a thirty-minute workout on a rowing machine. Since most moms can't find an extra thirty minutes each day (or the rowing machine, for that matter, since it's buried under the laundry), why not find three minutes today to laugh with your kids.

Because kids can spot a manufactured moment in a heartbeat, let the fun happen naturally. If it's cold and snowy—go outside. Make snow angels. Take a spray bottle of colored water with you, so kids can paint their angel or decorate a snowman. On a warm, sunny day be silly and pretend it's winter. Give your kids a shaker full of flour and let them powder everything in sight (the rain will wash it away). Or, let the kids wash their bicycles while you wash the car. Use a hose and a bucket so you can have a water fight, too. Rainy day fun and laughter is possible by making tents out of blankets, chairs, and tables. Read, nap, or giggle in those makeshift tents. Keep a stock of balloons on hand, too. Blow them up, release them, and giggle together as they fly across the room.

You're in charge of making your family's memories, so let them be fun ones. Let God's joy, laughter, and happiness pervade your life and home. Remember, one day you may end up in a portrait atop a piano. Will you be a sepia relation in black crepe or a smiling mom surrounded by laughing kids? The choice is yours.

I Will

Delight in the life God has given me.	*yes*	*no*
Model God's character of joy, laughter, and happiness.	*yes*	*no*
Let fun happen naturally in my home.	*yes*	*no*
Try to set aside a few moments every day to laugh.	*yes*	*no*
Remember that I am in charge of my family's memories of fun and laughter.	*yes*	*no*
Remind myself that playtime and laughter can be fun ways to become fit.	*yes*	*no*
Encourage my kids to lighten up, laugh, and have fun.	*yes*	*no*

Things to Do

 Make common kitchen objects into weird hats. Parade around the house wearing your fun-derful creations.

Read Job 8:1–21 to see how repentance can lead to laughter.

For fun let children paint themselves and the bathtub with water-based finger paint. Rinse clean when done.

Let your child use your old clothes for dress up. Take photos and laugh together.

If an old appliance is scheduled for the trash, let your kids have fun tearing it apart.

Go online and do some research to learn about the health benefits of laughter.

Things to Remember

Our mouths were filled with laughter, our tongues with songs of joy. Then it was said among the nations, "The LORD has done great things for them."

PSALM 126:2 NIV

Blessed are you who hunger now, for you shall be filled. Blessed are you who weep now, for you shall laugh.

LUKE 6:21 NKJV

To a person who is good in His sight He has given wisdom and knowledge and joy.

ECCLESIASTES 2:26 NASB

Light is sown like seed for the righteous and gladness for the upright in heart.

PSALM 97:11 NASB

You make the path of life known to me. In your presence there is complete joy.

ACTS 2:28 GOD'S WORD

Go eat your food and enjoy it; drink your wine and be happy, because that is what God wants you to do.

ECCLESIASTES 9:7 NCV

Let laughter reign when it comes. It is oil for the engines that rise to challenges and work miracles.

—DONALD E. DEMARAY

A sense of humor can help you overlook the unattractive, tolerate the unpleasant, cope with the unexpected, and smile through the unbearable.

—MOSE WALDOKS

Guidance

Which Way?

This God is our God forever and ever. He will guide us from now on. —PSALM 48:14 NCV

"Which way do we go? Which way do we go?" Two gangly vultures keep asking each other this question throughout a cartoon version of Rudyard Kipling's *The Jungle Book*. The constant repetition sets small children giggling as the vultures finally pull out a map to figure out which way to go.

Sometimes life's situations fit that easy formula—come to a crossroads, consult a map, and move ahead with certainty that this is the right way to go. Jeremiah 6:16 puts it this way: "Stand in the ways and see, And ask for the old paths, where the good way is, And walk in it; Then you will find rest for your souls" (NKJV). Simply stated this means when you come to a decision point in life, stop and look around. Ask for help, beginning with a prayer for God's guidance. Then turn to a mothering mentor. Rely on her honesty, wisdom, discernment, and encouragement to determine which way to go. You may not learn everything you need to know from one person. So consult a pastor or a parent, too.

God's Word reminds you "without counsel, plans go awry, but in the multitude of counselors they are established" (Proverbs 15:22 NKJV). What you learn from each advisor can be helpful and may be even life changing. Compare the advice from your counselors and move in the direction they suggest.

While this is a valid way to find guidance in most situations, sometimes life throws you a curve, leaving you alone or frightened. You "ask for the old paths, where the good way is," but you get several different answers. Now *you're* the responsible adult. You've seen the ripples on a pond when you've tossed in a stone. You know deep down the decision you make will affect someone—a child, a spouse, a family member, a friend. You must choose. But what do you do? Which way do you go?

When the path is dark and you're confused about a course of action, begin again with prayer. Remember that God has promised to be with you always. His constant presence means you can ask Him for help and wisdom and guidance and direction at any time. Center your thoughts by asking God to show you what resources you have available to you at this time—family, friends, monetary resources, places of safety or for counsel. Ask Him to show you what your choices are in the situation. No matter the size of the mountain, there are usually several ways to scale the summit. Then pray for clarity to see which choice is best and why you should make it. This way of praying for guidance and discernment is tough work. It requires thought and careful study. It takes time, too; so don't rush into a solution. Pray and then wait. Give God time to show you what to do. Then move out in faith, trusting Him to show you each step to take.

Consider this. When you walk down a darkened road in the middle of the night without moonlight or a streetlight lighting your way, you're liable to stumble. Even a small beam of light from a flashlight or lantern can make a walk in the dark much safer and make each footstep secure. God's guidance can become that beam of light for you in the darkness of decision.

As you actively seek God's guidance in the decisions you make, your example will light a path for your children to follow, too. When your children stand at crossroads in their lives, your example, guidance, kind words, and correction will help them make good decisions. You can remind them to submit their concerns to God in prayer, communicate any concerns about their decisions, explain rationally and patiently the situation as you view it, and offer your confidence in their ability to make good choices. Moms can't always make kids do what is right, but you can shine a light on their path and point out the best way for your children to go.

"Which way do we go?" The answer is clear. Seek out wise counselors; wait for God to show you clear direction; trust Him to guide you each step of the way. "Which way do we go?" Let's go God's way.

I Will

Remember God's constant presence with me.

    yes   _no_

Trust God to guide me as I make decisions for me and my children.

    yes   _no_

Consider the honesty, wisdom, and discernment of those persons I ask for advice.

    yes   _no_

Be aware that God's answers to my guidance questions may take some time.

    yes   _no_

Understand that there may be more than one solution to a problem.

    yes   _no_

Concede that my example and kind words can help guide my children to good decisions.

    yes   _no_

Things to Do

☐ *Glue cotton balls together to make a sheep-y reminder that God is your guiding shepherd.*

☐ *Set up a play date with a mentoring mom for insight and guidance in mothering.*

☐ *Make a list of decisions you need to make. Pray about them. Record God's answers.*

☐ *When making family decisions, let children give input. Consider their ideas seriously.*

☐ *Pray this with your kids: Lord guide me as I go; show me what I need to know.*

☐ *Get a good night's rest before making major decisions to ensure a clear mind.*

Things to Remember

The LORD will guide you continually, and satisfy your soul in drought, and strengthen your bones; you shall be like a watered garden, and like a spring of water.

ISAIAH 58:11 NKJV

Trust in the LORD with all your heart, and lean not on your own understanding; in all your ways acknowledge Him, and He shall direct your paths.

PROVERBS 3:5–6 NKJV

You are my rock and my fortress; for Your name's sake You will lead me and guide me.
Psalm 31:3 NASB

I am the LORD your God, who teaches you to do what is good, who leads you in the way you should go.

ISAIAH 48:17 NCV

Whether you turn to the right or to the left, your ears will hear a voice behind you, saying, "This is the way; walk in it."

ISAIAH 30:21 NIV

With unfailing love you will lead this people whom you have ransomed. You will guide them in your strength to the place where your holiness dwells.

EXODUS 15:13 NLT

When He, the Spirit of truth, has come,
He will guide you into all truth.

JOHN 16:13 NKJV

Show me Your ways, O LORD; teach me
Your paths. Lead me in Your truth and
teach me, for You are the God of my
salvation.

PSALM 25:4–5 NKJV

He will teach us his ways, so that we
may walk in his paths.

ISAIAH 2:3 NIV

The LORD says, "I will make you wise
and show you where to go. I will guide
you and watch over you."

PSALM 32:8 NCV

Teach me to do Your will, for You are
my God; Your Spirit is good. Lead me in
the land of uprightness.

PSALM 143:10 NKJV

He guards the course of the just and
protects the way of his faithful ones.

PROVERBS 2:8 NIV

God will, some way
or other, direct the
steps of those who
acknowledge him in
all their ways and
seek unto him for
direction with full
purpose of heart to
follow it.

—MATTHEW HENRY

What He will do, if
you will trust Him
and go cheerfully
ahead when He
shows you the way,
is to guide you still
farther.

—HORACE BUSHNELL

God's Provision

My Shepherd

The Lord *is my shepherd. I have everything I need.*

—Psalm 23:1 NCV

Psalm 23 is probably the best-loved passage in God's Word. Small children can find security in this assurance of God's care, and the aged or infirm facing death can find hope and comfort in the promise of God's presence. For Christian moms who spend a lifetime shepherding their children onto right paths, Psalm 23 paints a wonderful picture of a good shepherd who provides for His flock, who guides His lambs and keeps them safe. What an uplifting promise of God's never-ending care.

When David penned this psalm he wrote from personal experience. He knew the care he gave his sheep mirrored God's provision for him personally. David provided food, water, rest, and safety for his flock just as God provided those things for him. But God's care for the young shepherd boy extended beyond physical needs. Psalm 23 indicates that God also shepherded David spiritually—guiding him to make good choices, assuring him of His presence when David was afraid, loving David beyond all understanding, and promising him a home in heaven.

The blessing of Psalm 23 doesn't end with David. God wants to be your personal shepherd, too, to provide you with more than the physical needs of food, water, rest, safety, and strength. God wants to love you, guide you, be with you, and provide comfort and assurance for your heart, for you are far more important to God than a baaing ewe or fluffy lamb—you are God's child.

As God's child, you're never alone. God is with you. You can talk to Him, depend on Him, ask Him for the strength, wisdom, and guidance you need to mother your kids. Do you lack a job, food, money? God can provide—just ask. Do you need patience, comfort, creativity? God can meet those needs in the blink of an eye—speak up. Do your children need good friends, understanding teachers, new tennis shoes? God can take care of all of those things. God's provision is unlimited.

His Word says He will give you "richly all things to enjoy" (1 Timothy 6:17 NKJV), too, so ask Him. Trust Him. Wait for Him to provide (that's the hardest part for many moms, too). God wants to bless you and your children in ways you can't even imagine. Let Him shepherd you with His never-ending care. The lessons you learn from your heavenly shepherd will help you care for and shepherd your children, too.

I Will

Tell God my needs and trust Him to provide them.   yes _____   no _____

Teach my children that everything we have comes
from God.   yes _____   no _____

Believe that God wants to bless me.   yes _____   no _____

Rejoice in God's promise of His never-ending care.   yes _____   no _____

Try to be patient when waiting for God to provide for
me and my family.   yes _____   no _____

Remember to thank God for all His blessings.   yes _____   no _____

Look for opportunities to share with others about
the ways God has provided for me.   yes _____   no _____

Things to Do

 With your children make an alphabetical list of things God has provided for you.

 Read Exodus 15:22—16:35 with your kids. Discuss how God provided for His people.

 Keep a prayer journal this week of your requested needs and God's answers.

Draw and cut out sheep. Print Psalm 23:1 on them for your children to wear.

Ask an older Christian how God has provided for him or her over the years.

 Play the God Provides game. Name things that God will and will not give you.

Things to Remember

The LORD shall preserve you from all evil; He shall preserve your soul. The LORD shall preserve your going out and your coming in.

PSALM 121:7–8 NKJV

He is our God and we are the people he takes care of and the sheep that he tends.

PSALM 95:7 NCV

It is better to trust in the LORD than to put confidence in man. It is better to trust in the LORD than to put confidence in princes.

PSALM 118:8–9 NKJV

Ask, and God will give to you. Search, and you will find. Knock, and the door will open for you.

MATTHEW 7:7 NCV

God can give you more blessings than you need. Then you will always have plenty of everything—enough to give to every good work.

2 CORINTHIANS 9:8 NCV

The life of every creature and the breath of all people are in God's hand.

JOB 12:10 NCV

A God wise enough to create me and the world I live in is wise enough to watch out for me.

—PHILIP YANCEY

Our gracious God not only leads us in the way of mercy, but he prepares our path before us, providing for all our wants even before they occur.

—CHARLES SPURGEON

Growing Up Spiritually

Maturing Taste Buds

As newborn babes, desire the pure milk of the word, that you may grow thereby. —1 PETER 2:2 NKJV

There's nothing more touching than the sight of a newborn nestled in a mom's arms, eagerly sucking its milk. Milk is the first building block to growth—both physically and spiritually. Bible study and prayer are the milk your spirit needs to grow. God's Word says a Christian should "desire God's pure word as newborn babies desire milk. Then you will grow in your salvation" (1 Peter 2:2 GOD'S WORD).

However, kids need more than milk to grow. Everyone knows teenagers don't get their nourishment from a bottle of baby formula—they drink *their* milk directly from the carton inside the refrigerator as they wash down every piece of solid food in sight. Milk *and* solid food are necessary to a child's physical development. Moms move kids up from milk to cereal to strained foods because moms know kids need these foods to grow strong. To continue your spiritual growth you need to follow some rules, too. God's Word says "milk is for beginners, inexperienced in God's ways; solid food is for the mature, who have some practice in telling right from wrong" (Hebrews 5:13–14 THE MESSAGE).

To add some solid food to your regular Bible reading and prayer time, try using a prayer journal. Record your concerns and God's answers to make yourself more aware of God's work in your daily life. In addition, times when you get together to share and pray with other believers will grow your faith as you hear of God's faithfulness and provision. Connecting on a regular basis with another believer will help keep you accountable to growing in your faith, too.

Accomplishments in your children's lives accompany their physical growth—rolling over at six months; taking their first steps at ten months; leaving for their first day of school. As you grow in your faith you'll note spiritual accomplishments, too, like times when you can draw on your faith experiences and share them to help others grow. As you commit to moving ahead in your spiritual growth, like a runner training for a marathon, bulk up on your faith carbs by memorizing God's Word, leading a Bible study, or mentoring a new Christian.

So grow as your kids do. Start with the milk of God's Word, but don't stop there. Follow a few spiritual rules and watch your faith grow strong all life long.

I Will

Rejoice in the knowledge that I can grow in my faith.

yes _no_

Understand that growing in my spiritual life is a lifelong process.

yes _no_

Commit to growing beyond spiritual infancy to mature faith.

yes _no_

Realize that there are practical things I can do to grow in my faith.

yes _no_

Trust that God will help me grow in my spiritual life.

yes _no_

Recognize that my relationships with other believers can lead me to deeper faith.

yes _no_

Things to Do

☐ *Join a Bible study at your church to grow in your faith.*

☐ *Take your kids and visit your birthplace. Share some of your memories of growing up.*

☐ *Train to run in a race as a reminder of the training needed for spiritual growth.*

☐ *Post and use a growth chart. Note one accomplishment alongside each child's height, too.*

☐ *Find an accountability partner. Tell her about your desire and plans to expand your faith.*

☐ *Serve your kids some baby food. Thank God together that they've grown and can eat pizza.*

Things to Remember

If anyone believes in me, rivers of living water will flow out from that person's heart, as the Scripture says.

JOHN 7:38 NCV

You shall walk after the LORD your God and fear Him, and keep His commandments and obey His voice; you shall serve Him and hold fast to Him.

DEUTERONOMY 13:4 NKJV

I keep trying to reach the goal and get the prize for which God called me through Christ to the life above.

PHILIPPIANS 3:14 NCV

Those who live only to satisfy their own sinful desires will harvest the consequences of decay and death. But those who live to please the Spirit will harvest everlasting life.

GALATIANS 6:8 NLT

People who do what is true come to the light so that the things they do for God may be clearly seen.

JOHN 3:21 GOD'S WORD

Those who live following the Spirit are thinking about the things the Spirit wants them to do.

ROMANS 8:5 NCV

If I keep praying and asking God to make me to be what He wants me to be, some day I will be what I need to be.

—FRANCES KELLEY

Good principles fixed in the head will produce good resolutions in the heart and good practices in the life.

—MATTHEW HENRY

Trust

Go Ahead–Jump

Those who know Your name will put their trust in You.

—PSALM 9:10 NKJV

A little girl balanced on the edge of the neighborhood swimming pool. Her mother stood in the shallow water, urging her daughter to jump in, reassuring the child that she would be there to catch her. The little girl's eyes flickered back and forth between her mother's face and the water's sparkling wetness. The mother began to sing softly, "Trust and obey, for there's no other way to be happy in Jesus . . ." The mother paused, and the little girl smiled. Finishing the final phrase of the familiar hymn "Trust and Obey," the girl jumped into her mom's embrace.

All the little girl needed when facing that fearful jump was a reminder to trust. Once that cue was fresh in her mind, fear was gone. That's what God wants for you, too. He wants you to trust Him so completely that your fears melt away. He has promised to take care of you, to provide for you, to be with you and help you always. It's easy to remember and believe God will take care of you when life is good, when the bills have all been paid, when nobody in the family is sick, when you feel secure in your job. But what happens when something sends your good times into a tailspin? Can you jump into God's arms and trust Him to catch you and take care of you then?

There are many things that can keep a mom poised on the edge of fear. The media is full of bad news, war and falling stock prices, unemployment and rising crime rates. Some mothers are consumed with concerns about the future for their children in such a troubled world. Other moms live in fear that their children will be injured in an accident. There are unknown harms and hurts, too. Yet for all a mom's fears, the word that can wash over her soul and chase those fears away is trust. In the face of whatever might happen, a mom can toss her children into God's arms and trust Him to catch them and care for them.

Remember the Bible story about Joseph? His jealous brothers sold him into slavery when he was only a teenager. Taken to a strange land, he was wrongly accused and thrown into prison. But no matter what happened to him, Genesis 37 says Joseph trusted God. He had the firm conviction, belief, hope, and expectation that God would not abandon him, that God would keep His promises and take care of him. That's trust. God rewarded Joseph for his trust, too, in amazing ways. The awkward teen one day became the second-in-command to the Pharaoh of Egypt.

Yet the rewards for Joseph's trust didn't materialize overnight. Joseph struggled for many years, living in abysmal conditions in the jail. Fellow prisoners promised to say a kind word for him when they were released, but failed to follow through on their pledges. Though it must have seemed futile, Joseph kept trusting God. Year after year, Joseph would trustingly jump into God's arms, and even without anything tangible to prove it, year after year God caught him and cared for him. Through those awful years God taught Joseph and trained him so that when he was released Joseph was ready to trust God again to help him govern a nation.

Trusting God can become a daily habit. To learn to trust God all the time like Joseph did, begin trusting Him when life is easy. Count on God with a firm conviction and expectation that He will take care of everything in your life. Then, when trouble does come, *and it will*, it will be easier to stare down your fears and say, "God will take care of me." Pray about small things first, asking God to provide parking spaces or paper towels on sale when you really need them. Watching God provide for these little things will boost your trust in His ability to care for the bigger things, too, like paying for your kids' college tuition or finding a caregiver for aging parents. Remember when you trust God, you're not leaving anything to chance. His Word says, "the everlasting God is your place of safety, and His arms will hold you up forever" (Deuteronomy 33:27 NCV). So, go ahead—jump.

I Will

Ask God to help me trust Him as a little child.
_____ yes _____ no

Believe that nothing can happen to me that God isn't already handling.
_____ yes _____ no

Quit worrying about my children and trust God to care for them.
_____ yes _____ no

Confess to God when my trust in Him falters or fails.
_____ yes _____ no

Remember that it takes time to work through life's problems.
_____ yes _____ no

Accept that God has a purpose for all the days of my life.
_____ yes _____ no

Things to Do

☐ *Let your children jump off a step. Catch them, and talk about trust.*

☐ *Draw a hand; print IN GOD'S HAND on the palm and TRUST on the fingers.*

☐ *Read Daniel 3 to your children. Discuss how the three men trusted God.*

☐ *Talk with an older Christian about what makes trust in God grow stronger.*

☐ *List five things you fear. Commit them to God; then tear up the list.*

☐ *Do something you've never tried before because fear held you back.*

☐ *Make up a song for Nahum 1:7. Sing it often to remember to trust God.*

Things to Remember

The LORD is my strength and my shield; my heart trusts in him, and I am helped.

PSALM 28:7 NIV

The LORD is good, a refuge in times of trouble. He cares for those who trust in him.

NAHUM 1:7 NIV

Commit your way to the LORD, trust also in Him,
and He shall bring it to pass.
Psalm 37:5 KJV

I trust God, so I am not afraid. What can human beings do to me?

PSALM 56:4 NCV

O Sovereign LORD, you are God! Your words are trustworthy, and you have promised these good things to your servant.

2 SAMUEL 7:28 NIV

The fear of man brings a snare, but whoever trusts in the LORD shall be safe.

PROVERBS 29:25 NKJV

The Scripture says, "Whoever believes in Him will not be disappointed."

ROMANS 10:11 NASB

Those who are attentive to a matter will prosper, and happy are those who trust in the LORD.

PROVERBS 16:20 NRSV

This is what the LORD says: "Cursed are those who put their trust in mere humans and turn their hearts away from the LORD."

JEREMIAH 17:5 NLT

Some trust in chariots and some in horses, but we trust in the name of the LORD our God.

PSALM 20:7 NIV

Trust in the LORD, and do good; dwell in the land, and feed on His faithfulness.

PSALM 37:3 NKJV

Those who trust in the LORD are like Mount Zion, which cannot be moved, but abides forever.

PSALM 125:1 NKJV

He who trusts in himself is lost. He who trusts in God can do all things.

—ALPHONSAS LIGUORI

We have heard of many people who trusted God too little, but have you ever heard of anyone who trusted Him too much?

—J. HUDSON TAYLOR

Contentment

Madison Avenue Madness

My share in life has been pleasant; my part has been beautiful. —Psalm 16:6 NCV

What mom hasn't had to deal with a child who believes the media advertising, "You can't live without this . . ."? Whether it's a pair of shoes, an improved breakfast cereal, or the latest video game, the wants and whines of discontent echo throughout retail store aisles. It seems a Madison Avenue madness has taken over today's kids.

Unfortunately, discontent has haunted people since creation. Discontent drove Eve to eat the forbidden fruit. Discontent made the ancient Israelites complain about God's provision for them in the wilderness. In more recent times, discontent has fueled wars, torn marriages and families apart, and increased national and personal debt loads.

That's a lot of bad news—but here's the good. Contentment is possible. The apostle Paul says so. After being beaten and imprisoned Paul said, "I have learned to be satisfied with the things I have and with everything that happens" (Philippians 4:11 NCV). The secret to Paul's contentment? A strong focus on God. Paul knew from experience that contentment is not found in people, places, or possessions. True contentment comes from putting God first and everything else second.

Sounds easy, but it's hard to do when you're surrounded by the I-wants. Fads capitalize on a child's need for acceptance by peers. Unfortunately, once a kid acquires the all-important item of the moment, something else is sure to beckon. To spare your wallet and your child from the pressures of unneeded purchases, look at the things you already own. If your possessions (including your kids' things) were destroyed tomorrow, what items would be at the top of your must replace list? Consider whether you would merely *want* those items replaced or truly *need* them.

Set some shopping rules for your family, too. Discuss the expense of being on the cutting edge of fashion. Determine how much stuff is enough and how much stuff is too much. Contrary to a popular bumper sticker, the one who has the most stuff when they die doesn't win anything. They just leave a mess behind for other people to deal with.

So find contentment God's way. Look for Him in every moment, every opportunity, every decision. Stuff the Madison Avenue madness of discontent, and replace it instead with godly contentment, remembering "since we entered the world penniless and will leave it penniless, if we have bread on the table and shoes on our feet, that's enough" (1 Timothy 6:7–8 THE MESSAGE).

I Will

Remember that contentment comes from an inner attitude, not outer assets.

yes _no_

Ask God to help me be content with the things He has given me.

yes _no_

Follow Paul's example and focus more on God than on people, places, and possessions.

yes _no_

Realize how destructive discontent can be to my family and me.

yes _no_

Choose to put God first and everything else second to find true contentment.

yes _no_

Commit to spending more time on people and less money on things.

yes _no_

Things to Do

☐ _List as many blessings as you and your kids can name in three minutes._

☐ _With your kids, volunteer at a neighborhood food pantry and watch your discontent disappear._

☐ _Read Numbers 11. Discuss the Israelites' complaints and God's provision._

☐ _Listen to media advertising for a day. List advertised items that are absolutely necessary for life._

☐ _Make an acrostic from the word "content." Let each letter stand for something about God._

☐ _Serve your family rice for breakfast, lunch, and supper. Thank God for your well-stocked pantry._

Things to Remember

Let your conduct be without covetousness; be content with such things as you have.

HEBREWS 13:5 NKJV

Give me neither poverty nor riches, but give me only my daily bread.

PROVERBS 30:8 NIV

I have learned to be satisfied with the things I have and with everything that happens.

PHILIPPIANS 4:11 NCV

Far better to be right and poor than to be wrong and rich.

PROVERBS 16:8 THE MESSAGE

It is better to be poor and respect the LORD than to be wealthy and have much trouble.

PROVERBS 15:16 NCV

Godliness with contentment is great gain. For we brought nothing into this world, and it is certain we can carry nothing out. And having food and clothing, with these we shall be content.

1 TIMOTHY 6:6–8 NKJV

True contentment is the power of getting out of any situation all that there is in it.
—G. K. CHESTERTON

When the heart is content to be without the outward blessing, it is as happy as it would be with it, for it is as rest.
—CHARLES SPURGEON

Loss

A Corn Dolly's Lesson

Blessed are those who mourn, for they shall be comforted.
—MATTHEW 5:4 NKJV

Every girl in the 1860s probably played with a two-headed corn dolly. Both ends of a dried corncob were carved with faces—one smiling, the other sad. A reversible skirt was attached at the middle of the corncob. The side nearest the happy face sported bright fabrics; the reverse fabric was always black. By hiding either end of the corncob in the reversible skirt, girls could imagine their dolls in both happy and sad situations. Because many families experienced war-related deaths at this time, the dolls helped young girls deal with loss and grief.

Unfortunately, loss is a part of life that you and your children will experience. Feelings of loss accompany the death of a relative or favorite pet. Loss will tug at your heart when friends move away. It's also tough to face the loss of a game, or when dreams or a favorite toy are broken and cannot be fixed. As your children get older, the end of relationships or a divorce can be as upsetting as the loss of self-esteem for not making the team or being accepted into a particular college. Such losses cause some teens to be depressed or commit suicide.

Loss is hard to bear, but it doesn't have to keep you down. Just as girls could flip that corn dolly from sad to happy, God's Word reminds you that loss can be turned into something good, too. When a believer dies, take heart. God promises that one day His children will rise to a glorious life with Him. The apostle Paul adds that other life losses can become lessons in compassion, too, as you share with others the comfort you've received from God in your times of loss.

Be careful when loss comes your way. When playing a game, let your children learn from your example how to be a gracious loser. If you anticipate the death of someone dear to you, give your children an opportunity to say good-bye. Attend the funeral together, if they're old enough. Let your children gather solemnly to share recollections of a pet that has died. Plant a seed to illustrate the good that can come from losing something, reminding children that the seed must die in order for a plant to grow. If a child exhibits symptoms of depression, talk to a pastor or medical professional. Remember, God is still God despite life's losses. Let Him comfort you and your children and turn the loss to good.

I Will

Understand that loss is a part of life that my children and I will experience.

<u>*yes*</u>   <u>*no*</u>

Admit that loss can have long-lasting emotional consequences.

<u>*yes*</u>   <u>*no*</u>

Recall that losing a game can be as devastating to children as losing a pet.

<u>*yes*</u>   <u>*no*</u>

Be thankful for God's promises to be with me in times of loss and grief.

<u>*yes*</u>   <u>*no*</u>

Know that God's comfort can flow from me to others in their times of loss.

<u>*yes*</u>   <u>*no*</u>

Be aware that loss affects different people in different ways.

<u>*yes*</u>   <u>*no*</u>

Things to Do

☐ *Write a poem about someone who died, mentioning his or her accomplishments and other good memories.*

☐ *Wander through a cemetery. Read the tombstone engravings to ease your children's fear of death.*

☐ *Plant five tomato seeds. Discuss how seeds must die to let plants grow.*

☐ *Play a favorite game. Have everyone try to lose. The best loser wins.*

☐ *Make a list of things that would be good to lose—such as extra weight or mosquitoes.*

☐ *Talk to a mentor mom and asked how she handled the losses in her life.*

Things to Remember

The LORD gave, and the LORD has taken away; blessed be the name of the LORD.

JOB 1:21 NKJV

I will never forget this awful time, as I grieve over my loss. Yet I still dare to hope when I remember this: The unfailing love of the LORD never ends!

LAMENTATIONS 3:20–22 NLT

Nothing—nothing living or dead, angelic or demonic, today or tomorrow, high or low, thinkable or unthinkable— absolutely nothing can get between us and God's love.

ROMANS 8:38–39 THE MESSAGE

You hear, O LORD, the desire of the afflicted; you encourage them, and you listen to their cry.

PSALM 10:17 NIV

The LORD is near to those who have a broken heart, and saves such as have a contrite spirit.

PSALM 34:18 NKJV

God is the Father who is full of mercy and all comfort. He comforts us every time we have trouble, so when others have trouble, we can comfort them.

2 CORINTHIANS 1:3–4 NCV

When circumstances are against us, we must be able to set the sails of our souls and use even adverse winds.

—E. STANLEY JONES

God gives His children the capacity to empathize, to understand, by bringing similar sufferings into our lives.

—CHARLES SWINDOLL

Worry

Anxious Meditation

The LORD himself will go before you . . . Don't be afraid and don't worry. —DEUTERONOMY 31:8 NCV

Here's a riddle for moms: What do going to the dentist, to kindergarten, and to sleep in an unfamiliar place have in common? Besides the obvious answer that each situation involves going to something, each situation can also be worrisome. New problems, new people, and new places all come with unknowns that can cause big worries for little kids.

Moms do a lot of worrying, too. When you think about a verse from God's Word, or consider a point from the pastor's sermon, turning the thought over in your mind and reviewing it from all angles, that's meditating on God. But, when you think about a problem or concern from all angles, turning it over in your mind to figure out how to make it work, make it better, or make it go away, that's not meditating—that's worrying. Sometimes worry and fear walk hand in hand. Worrying about your kids' safety, going over the what-ifs from every angle, can lead to a fearful, overprotective attitude that could prevent your child from learning or growing through new situations.

To spare your kids unnecessary worries, begin watching your words. Your conversations about which teacher your child will have in kindergarten or how much you hate visiting the dentist can be a source of major worry for a five-year-old, especially if he or she has heard stories about how "mean" a teacher is or how painful a dentist's visit can be.

Be observant around your children, too. Watch their body language. When worried, children may act like a nylon slip with static cling, wrapping themselves around your legs. Happy or playful distractions—singing a song with hand motions, for example—can sometimes break the weight of worry for little ones. Ask an older child to imagine the worst possible thing that could happen and make up a rap or song about it. Bedtime worries can be soothed with a regular ritual—a tickle fest followed with a song or story, a stuffed animal or a soft blanket to hug, and a prayer and some kisses, both on the forehead and one wrapped inside a palm for use whenever your little one needs a kiss during the night.

Above all, to spare your family from anxiety, take your worries to God in prayer first before anxiety can take a hold on your emotions. He has promised to take care of you, and replace your worries with peace. And what God says, He'll do. You don't have to worry about that.

I Will

Understand worry is contagious and can spread to my kids through my words and actions.

yes _____ no _____

Be aware that unresolved worry can lead to fear.

yes _____ no _____

Take my worries and concerns to God in prayer.

yes _____ no _____

Trust God to guide me through worrisome times and situations.

yes _____ no _____

Thank God for His promises of peace, care, and comfort.

yes _____ no _____

Prayerfully watch for the warning signs of worry in my children.

yes _____ no _____

Things to Do

☐ *Read Matthew 6:25–34. List the things God says not to worry about.*

☐ *To dispel nighttime worries, leave bedroom doors open a bit and nightlights on.*

☐ *Keep one or two funny, happy videos to watch during stormy nights or worrisome times.*

☐ *Read library books about the new situations facing your kids to help calm their worries.*

☐ *Write kids' worries in chalk on the driveway. Pray about them, and wash them away.*

☐ *Call another mom and share your worries with her. Ask for her prayers, too.*

Things to Remember

Do not worry about anything, but pray and ask God for everything you need, always giving thanks.

PHILIPPIANS 4:6 NCV

Do not worry, saying, "What shall we eat?" or "What shall we drink?" or "What shall we wear?" . . . Your heavenly Father knows that you need all these things.

MATTHEW 6:31–32 NKJV

Be still, and know that I am God; I will be exalted among the nations, I will be exalted in the earth! The LORD of hosts is with us.

PSALM 46:10–11 NKJV

Do not worry about your life, what you will eat or what you will drink; nor about your body, what you will put on. Is not life more than food?

MATTHEW 6:25 NKJV

Cast your burden on the LORD, and He shall sustain you; He shall never permit the righteous to be moved.

PSALM 55:22 NKJV

Don't worry about tomorrow, because tomorrow will have its own worries. Each day has enough trouble of its own.

MATTHEW 6:34 NCV

Worry only destroys the effectiveness of lives that would otherwise be useful and beautiful.

—DARLOW SARGEANT

Anxiety is not only a pain which we must ask God to assuage but also a weakness we must ask him to pardon—for he's told us to take no care for the morrow.

—C. S. LEWIS

Asking for Help

Supermom

The Lord is for me; he will help me. —Psalm 118:7 NLT

A poster on a church bulletin board proclaimed: "Dear Lord, so far today I've done all right. I haven't gossiped, haven't lost my temper, haven't been greedy, grumpy, nasty, selfish, or overindulgent. I'm very thankful for that. But in a few minutes, Lord, I'm going to get out of bed. And from then on, I'm probably going to need a lot more help."

How true. Every day starts out as a good day, but all too often challenges of mothering can turn the sweetest mom into one of Snow White's little friends from the dark side: Grumpy, Angry, or Meanie. However, the bulletin board poster contains a punch line that packs a lesson for moms in challenging situations: Ask for help.

It sounds easy, but it's tough to do. Why? Christian moms often wear themselves out because of the supermom in Proverbs 31. This woman can do it all. Cooking, sewing, gardening, working outside the home—the list is endless. Everyone loves this woman; her husband and children called her blessed. The townspeople know who she is, too; her reputation is spotless. And everyone knows she did it all on her own, so you should, too, right? Wrong. If you've been trying to be like this supermom on your own, give yourself a break.

Consider the phrase in Proverbs 31:15 that says this supermom provides food "for her maidservants" (KJV). *Maidservants*—plural. Round the clock, live-in servants who were there to help get the paperwork done, the clothes washed, the grocery shopping finished, the kids ready for school, and the husband out the door to the office on time. Sure, this supermom had to be organized, had to be a good manager, had to be out of bed before noon, but think about this: you can still be a Proverbs 31 mom and have help, too. All you have to do is ask.

Start with prayer. Before your feet hit the ground each morning, ask for God's help to care for your family. Then consider the help you already have in your home—your kids, a spouse, or another family member. Talk with these live-in helpers. Ask for their support as you look for ways to share the household chores. Be fair in deciding who should do what. You can always divide the chores into chunks and let your helpers choose which chunk of chores they want to do—clean the bathroom and kitchen or do the laundry and grocery shopping. Then stand back and let them work, even if they don't do the chores the exact way you do. Your way may be different, but it's not the only way to get the job done.

Make sure all chores are appropriate to a child's age. If the chore-sharing starts when your kids are young, they'll be better prepared to live on their own when they leave home, too. So ask toddlers to help pick up toys, set and clear the table, and feed the pets. School age children can make their beds (maybe not as neatly as you can, though, so give them a puffy quilt to spread over the top of the wrinkled sheets and frumpy pillows). First and second graders can clean out their closets and tidy their rooms. By the time a child is nine or ten he or she should be able to clean the bathroom and vacuum the house. Job jars are good, too, as are charts with pictures and words so that all the kids can see who is doing what on which days.

You might want to trade responsibilities with your spouse or another mom, too. Each adult would have total care for all the kids one or two nights a week. This way you'll have a regular opportunity to do something you prefer to do on your night off—take a class, work late, go to the library. If you don't have a responsible adult to swap chores with, think about hiring a mother's helper who can come by during the day for several hours each week. She could do dishes, laundry, and light housework so that you can take care of other chores.

Every mom needs a helping hand, but don't wait for others to read your mind. Be a Proverbs 31 mom and ask for help when you need it.

I Will

Recognize that trying to be a supermom often leaves me worn out. ____ yes ____ no

Know that when I'm tired and overworked I'm not as nice as I should be. ____ yes ____ no

Accept that it will be hard to ask for help. ____ yes ____ no

Consider that asking for help means I'll have to relinquish being in charge of everything. ____ yes ____ no

Concede that another's way to do a task may be better than mine. ____ yes ____ no

Things to Do

☐ Set aside a family meeting time to discuss sharing household chores.

☐ Make a chart with words and pictures to help kids remember what to do when.

☐ Give each child a gold star for chores accomplished. Reward five stars with a treat.

☐ Post a sign on the refrigerator that says: "Have I asked for help today?"

☐ Make chores fun. You use the toy vacuum; your kids use the big one.

☐ Read Exodus 18:9–27. What can you learn from Moses and Jethro about asking for help?

☐ Ask a mothering mentor or grandmother what kinds of assistance have been helpful to them.

Things to Remember

I will provide for their needs before they ask, and I will help them while they are still asking for help.

ISAIAH 65:24 NCV

I say to you, ask, and it will be given to you; seek, and you will find; knock, and it will be opened to you.

LUKE 11:9 NKJV

Call upon Me in the day of trouble; I shall rescue you, and you will honor Me.
Psalm 50:15 NASB

Call to Me, and I will answer you, and show you great and mighty things, which you do not know.

JEREMIAH 33:3 NKJV

The LORD is close to all who call on him, yes, to all who call on him sincerely.

PSALM 145:18 NLT

You're going to wear yourself out—and the people, too. This job is too heavy a burden for you to handle all by yourself.

EXODUS 18:18 NLT

By helping each other with your troubles, you truly obey the law of Christ.

GALATIANS 6:2 NCV

Two people are better than one . . . If one falls down, the other can help him up. But it is bad for the person who is alone and falls, because no one is there to help.

ECCLESIASTES 4:9–10 NCV

He said, "I cried out to the LORD in my great trouble, and he answered me.

JONAH 2:2 NLT

Behold, God is my helper; the Lord is with those who uphold my life.

PSALM 54:4 KJV

I want us to help each other with the faith we have. Your faith will help me, and my faith will help you.

ROMANS 1:12 NCV

The LORD has heard my cry for help; the LORD will answer my prayer.

PSALM 6:9 NCV

If Moses couldn't handle all the needs of the Israelites alone, why do we think we can handle all the needs of those around us without help?

—ELISA MORGAN AND CAROL KUYKENDALL

You are coming to a king, large petitions with you bring; for his grace and power are such none can ever ask too much.

—JOHN NEWTON

Enough of the Enoughs

*Long life to you! Good health to you and your household!
And good health to all that is yours!*   —1 Samuel 25:6 NIV

Doctors, warning labels, and well-meaning neighbors remind pregnant women to take care of themselves. God's Word echoes those concerns, too, by reminding you your body is a "temple of the Holy Spirit" (1 Corinthians 6:19 KJV). When you were pregnant you probably took most of these reminders to heart and slept eight hours every night, ate a balanced diet, and enjoyed outdoor activities. Now, however, your days are ordered by the demands of an active child. Yet you both still need the three enough's—enough sleep, enough exercise, and enough good food—to keep you both going and growing.

Because feedings may occur as frequently as every two hours during an infant's first few months, sleep deprivation is often a constant companion. So sleep when you can. If possible, ask another family member to help with nighttime feedings and emergencies. Also, when it's naptime for junior, don't use those golden minutes to catch up on paperwork. Catch a catnap instead. As your child grows older there will still be interruptions to your sleep patterns, too, because of night noises, upset tummies, or a myriad of other miseries.

Make sure you set an early bedtime for both of you. Late nights make for tough mornings. You need your rest, and you may need naps, too. Let sleep energize you—even if it's only in fifteen-minute snatches.

Exercise will also help boost your power reserves. Though housework may burn calories, vacuuming and dusting won't give you the same health benefits as walking, biking, or jumping rope. Let the dust accumulate for another day and take a half-hour walk around the block while your little one pedals along on a bike or tricycle. Play a game of hopscotch before fixing supper. Take time for a hike on weekends, backpacking your little ones if necessary. Impatience and irritability rarely sprout when you and your child have had some active time together.

In addition to enough sleep and exercise, moms and kids need to eat good food to keep your hearts healthy and your bodies strong. An overdose of snacks filled with sugar and caffeine can bring on late-day fatigue and grouchiness that a suppertime peanut butter sandwich won't cure. For a body-and-heart-healthy diet that will keep everyone content between meals, try to work in three servings of dairy products, four fruits and vegetables, four breads or cereals, and two servings of meat or fish each day. A prayer of thanks before each meal will help keep your heart *spiritually* healthy, too.

I Will

Remind myself that my body is God's temple, to be honored and cared for.

yes _____ *no* _____

Remember that to stay alert and energized I need to get more sleep each day.

yes _____ *no* _____

Recognize that I need to eat balanced meals to stay heart healthy.

yes _____ *no* _____

Understand that by exercising regularly I can be a stronger, healthier mom.

yes _____ *no* _____

Concede that when I am healthy I am better able to care for my child.

yes _____ *no* _____

Things to Do

- [ ] *Make the kitchen table into a tent. Take a nap there with your toddler.*

- [ ] *Trade babysitting time with a neighbor. Use the quiet time to catch a quick nap.*

- [ ] *Require your kids to eat the same number of bites of vegetables as their age.*

- [ ] *List some healthy foods your children can eat whenever they want (such as fruit or cheese).*

- [ ] *For snack time, fill muffin tins with healthy finger foods (crackers, raw veggies, fruit).*

- [ ] *Take turns kicking a small rock in front of you as you take a walk.*

- [ ] *Race through the house, picking up and putting away five items. First one done, wins.*

Things to Remember

Listen carefully to Me, and eat what is good, and let your soul delight itself in abundance.

ISAIAH 55:2 NKJV

A cheerful look brings joy to the heart, and good news gives health to the bones.

PROVERBS 15:30 NIV

Training your body helps you in some ways, but serving God helps you in every way by bringing you blessings in this life and in the future life, too.

1 TIMOTHY 4:8 NCV

Don't depend on your own wisdom. Respect the LORD and refuse to do wrong. Then your body will be healthy, and your bones will be strong.

PROVERBS 3:7–8 NCV

You shall serve the LORD your God, and He will bless your bread and your water; and I will remove sickness from your midst.

EXODUS 23:25 NASB

Do you not know that your body is a temple of the Holy Spirit within you, which you have from God, and that you are not your own?

1 CORINTHIANS 6:19 NRSV

He who enjoys health is rich, though he knows it not.
—ITALIAN PROVERB

If you have [health], praise God, and value it next to a good conscience, for health is the second blessing that we mortals are capable of— a blessing that money cannot buy.
—IZAAK WALTON

Apron Time

---

*Oh come, let us worship and bow down; let us kneel before the L*ORD *our Maker.*   —PSALM 95:6 KJV

It had taken King Solomon seven years to build the temple in Jerusalem. All the elders, leaders, and families in Israel came to town for a dedication ceremony. The Ark of the Covenant was situated in the Most Holy Place. The priests were consecrated; musicians played. Yet it wasn't until the people began to worship God that "the glory of the LORD filled the house of God" (2 Chronicles 5:14 KJV). When the congregation's worship rose up to heaven, God's presence came down in abundance.

Worship was important in Solomon's day, and worship should be important to you, too. Worship—the adoration, devotion, and love of God—expresses reverence and praise for God's greatness. Worship voices your gratitude to God for His blessings. Worship brings God closer to you, too. God's Word says worship offered in spirit and truth pleases God; and, if people didn't worship God "the stones would immediately cry out."

Yet moms face challenges when it comes to worship. Though your heart may yearn for time spent with God, kids, chores, and more consume a significant amount of your time and energy each day. There's so much to do; you're so tired. Finding time to be with God seems impossible. But is it?

Susannah Wesley, mother of John and Charles, would have understood your dilemma. With fifteen children her days were quite full. But Susannah knew the value of a personal worship time. Every day she would pull her apron over her head as a signal to her children that she was spending time alone with God. Unusual? Definitely. But Susannah recognized true worship must fit your personality and lifestyle. You may be quiet and reserved when you worship, with or without an apron over your head like Susannah, or you may be spontaneous and dance through the house when you worship God, like King David did. Your style of worship might embarrass some people (the apron thing could look a little strange to the mailman), but God doesn't care about worship styles as long as you are sincere.

So don't neglect your personal worship time. Connect with your Creator every day: Pray while changing a diaper; dance your praise to God while vacuuming the house; shout snippets of Scripture while washing the dishes; sing a praise song during bath time—even if you sing out of tune. You can be present in your everyday duties and still enter God's presence.

In addition, busy moms and wiggly kids can worship God in their actions. John 12:3 says "Mary took a pound of very costly oil of spikenard, anointed the feet of Jesus, and wiped His feet with her hair" (KJV). Mary's *act* of worship was unmistakable. Using your gifts, talents, and abilities for God's glory can be *your* act of worship, too.

The icing on the cake of King Solomon's dedication ceremony was God's manifested presence when the people began to worship together. Worship time with other believers is also important for you and your children. And, if you want that worship time to be meaningful, make sure to prepare your heart in advance. Watch your commitments the night before church. Getting to bed too late will leave you yawning instead of yearning for God. Set aside the usual bustle of activities, chores, and to do lists. If you didn't get everything done before worship, let it wait for one more day.

Be careful how you come to church, too. Your attitude and spirit affect not only *your* worship, but also the worship of others. Rushing out the door, fighting in the car, and harsh words in the parking lot are worship killers for you and your family. Tune your car radio to praise music so that the commute time will turn your hearts to God. During the worship service show respect for God and each other. Remember that worship is all about God, not about your personal preferences over a worship style. Use your corporate worship time to give God honor and glory. Engage your heart, mind, and soul so that worship won't become a ritual. Give God your best. Come into His presence—and worship.

I Will

Acknowledge that God alone is worthy of my praise and worship.

yes _____ *no* _____

Allow the wonder of God to fill my heart and overflow into praise to Him.

yes _____ *no* _____

Remind myself to enter God's presence in worship as I carry out my everyday duties.

yes _____ *no* _____

Give God my best whenever I worship Him—whether in word or deed.

yes _____ *no* _____

Take a chance and try a new style of worship.

yes _____ *no* _____

Things to Do

☐ *When feeling weary, splash cool water on your face to remember the refreshment found in worship.*

☐ *Make up a praise dance and jig your way to joyful worship.*

☐ *Sing a praise song to God. Use kitchen items—pots, graters, spoons—as instruments.*

☐ *Fill one day's prayers with nothing but worship and praise—don't ask for anything.*

☐ *List five of God's characteristics that make Him worthy of your worship: good, faithful, loving, forgiving, fair.*

☐ *Copy Revelation 5:12 onto a card. Post this wonderful reminder on your bathroom mirror.*

☐ *Find crayons, markers, or paints. Let your children draw colorful pictures to illustrate Psalm 150.*

Things to Remember

You are a chosen generation, a royal priesthood, a holy nation, His own special people, that you may proclaim the praises of Him who called you out of darkness into His marvelous light.

1 PETER 2:9 KJV

Through Jesus let us always offer to God our sacrifice of praise, coming from lips that speak his name.

HEBREWS 13:15 NCV

Give praise and honor and glory to the King of heaven. Everything he does is right and fair.
Daniel 4:37 NCV

I will worship toward Your holy temple, and praise Your name for Your lovingkindness and Your truth.

PSALM 138:2 KJV

Give unto the LORD the glory due to His name; worship the LORD in the beauty of holiness.

PSALM 29:2 KJV

It is written in the Scriptures, "You must worship the Lord your God and serve only him."

MATTHEW 4:10 NCV

God is Spirit, and those who worship Him must worship in spirit and truth.

JOHN 4:24 KJV

The LORD lives! Blessed be my rock, and exalted be my God, the rock of my salvation.

2 SAMUEL 22:47 NRSV

Because Your lovingkindness is better than life, my lips shall praise You. Thus I will bless You while I live; I will lift up my hands in Your name.

PSALM 63:3–4 KJV

You, LORD, have made me glad through Your work; I will triumph in the works of Your hands.

PSALM 92:4 KJV

I will praise you forever for what you have done; in your name I will hope, for your name is good. I will praise you in the presence of your saints.

PSALM 52:9 NIV

All of you can join together with one voice, giving praise and glory to God, the Father of our Lord Jesus Christ.

ROMANS 15:6 NLT

We pay God honor and reverence, not for his sake (because he is of himself full of glory to which no creature can add anything), but for our own sake.

—SAINT THOMAS AQUINAS

Worship—the only gift we can bring to God that he himself has not first given to us.

—ISOBEL RALSTON

Setting an Example

Me and My Shadow

These commandments that I give you today are to be upon your hearts. Impress them on your children.

—DEUTERONOMY 6:6–7 NIV

Every mom cringes when she hears her child repeat in public some statement she has made in anger or with sarcasm. Young children have a particular knack for this embarrassing habit. Why do kids forget what you tell them to do, but remember the words or actions you'd prefer they forget? A simple reason: the shadow factor.

Your children probably enjoy playing with shadows—wiggling and waggling them . . . stomping on someone else's shadow . . . hiding their shadow in a larger one. Though playing with shadows is merely a game, it's a visual reminder of how your children view you, too. Your children will always follow in your shadow, for you are their example. They will imitate your movements, echo your words, and mold their shadows to your larger one by patterning their life choices after your example.

There's no getting around it, your children will imitate you. Genesis 20 and 26 tell the story of Abraham and the shadow he cast for his children. Abraham, fearful that the Philistines might kill him to take his wife, told them, "She is my sister." Years later, Abraham's son Isaac did exactly the same thing, claiming his wife was his sister. Abraham's cowardly lie produced a poor example for his son to follow. Though Abraham undoubtedly *told* Isaac many things about living life, it was Abraham's *example* that Isaac followed when the going got tough. Telling your children what to do is important, but teaching them by example is vital.

Casting a good shadow is hard, so God's Word offers some suggestions. To set a good example for your children, start by loving God above everything else. Try to please Him in everything you do. Your children imitate you because they love you and want to be like you. The same principle applies to your relationship with God. If you truly love Him, you'll read His Word; you'll follow His commands. Your children will see you "abide under the shadow of the Almighty" (Psalm 91:1 KJV); they'll want God's shadow to cover them, too.

Don't forget the apostle Paul's words: "Follow my example, as I follow the example of Christ" (1 Corinthians 11:1 NIV). When it comes to mothering your children, you need to find a mom or grandmom who casts a godly shadow. Follow her example. Christian radio shows and parenting books may serve as your examples, too. Your children *will* imitate you, so cast a shadow for them of a godly mom, following others who "follow the example of Christ."

I Will

Love God and follow His example in every area of
my life.

_____ yes   _____ no

Begin each day by committing my family into
God's hands.

_____ yes   _____ no

Relax and stop trying to be perfect.

_____ yes   _____ no

Ask God to help me cast a godly shadow.

_____ yes   _____ no

Trust God to change wrong attitudes to right ones.

_____ yes   _____ no

Fill my mind and heart with God's truths.

_____ yes   _____ no

Enjoy motherhood because I know God is in charge.

_____ yes   _____ no

Things to Do

☐ Read Deuteronomy 6:1–7 to find out what God expects of families.

☐ List the character traits you want your children to see modeled
in your life.

☐ Play with your child's shadow on a sunny day, remembering God's
shadow on your life.

☐ Print BE LIKE GOD TODAY on a card and put it on your mirror.

☐ Read the Bible every day this week. Start with the book of Matthew.

☐ Find a godly mom whose advice you can implement and whose
example you can follow.

☐ Discard ungodly influences in your home (magazines, videos, games).

Things to Remember

I have given you an example, that you should do as I have done to you.

JOHN 13:15 NKJV

Be imitators of God, therefore, as dearly loved children and live a life of love, just as Christ loved us.

EPHESIANS 5:1 NIV

In every way be an example by doing good deeds. When you teach, do it with honesty and seriousness. Speak the truth so that you cannot be criticized.

TITUS 2:7–8 NCV

I will be careful to lead a blameless life—when will you come to me? I will walk in my house with blameless heart.

PSALM 101:2 NIV

All of you should try to follow my example and to copy those who live the way we showed you.

PHILIPPIANS 3.17 NCV

Tell the older women to be reverent in behavior, not to be slanderers or slaves to drink; they are to teach what is good, so that they may encourage the young women.

TITUS 2:3–4 NRSV

Do not let your deeds belie your words, lest when you speak in church someone may say to himself, "Why do you not practice what you preach?"

—SAINT JEROME

The best thing to give to your enemy is forgiveness; to an opponent, tolerance; to a friend, your heart; to your child, a good example.

—ARTHUR JAMES BALFOUR

Faith

An Unexpected Boatload

We live by faith, not by sight. —2 CORINTHIANS 5:7 NIV

Luke 5:1–11 recounts a strange fish story. Peter, a professional fisherman, had fished all night long without success. Jesus came along and told him to go back out into deep water "and let down the nets for a catch" (Luke 5:4 NIV). Peter reminded Jesus that his luck hadn't been good the night before, but because Jesus said so, Peter faithfully cast off. Can you imagine the reaction of bystanders when Peter hauled in a boatload of fish? What a miracle.

Now imagine you've spent an entire day trying to settle squabbles between your toddlers or teens while attempting to clean the house, do the laundry, and stretch the money left in the checking account to cover the mountain of groceries that have to be purchased to keep everyone fed. You've just about torn your hair out, but along comes Jesus, walking along the shoreline of your hassles, suggesting that you jump right back into the middle of them. At this point you have a choice to make—and so did Peter. The true miracle illustrated in Luke 5 is not the unexpected boatload of fish. The deeper miracle was Peter's faith.

Think about it. Here was a man who fished for a living. He knew the habits of fish, the ins and outs of sunlight and water temperatures, and where to find the denizens of the deep. Along comes Jesus—a carpenter by trade and a preacher by God's calling—with instructions to fish where Peter is sure there are no fish to be found. Yet there is something in Jesus and in Peter that connect, something that prompts Peter to say, "All right. I'll give it a try." That something is faith.

You have that faith, too. You exercise it often without realizing it. Every time you plop down on a kitchen chair, you're exhibiting faith that the chair will hold you. Every time you place your head in the hands of a hairdresser, you're exhibiting faith in that individual's ability to turn your mop into a masterpiece. Every time you turn a car key, flip a light switch, or floss your back teeth you're exhibiting faith that your action will produce a desired result.

God wants you to have that kind of faith in Him, too. He wants you to rely on Him for everything you do, so that no matter what you face in your daily life as a mom you can trust Him with as much abandon as you do your favorite kitchen chair. God wants to connect with you like Jesus did with Peter so that when you're overwhelmed with mothering, feeling like there's no end in sight, you can look God squarely in the eye and plunge back into the middle of family life, hoping and trusting He'll set everything to rights.

How do you get that connection, that faith in God? God's Word says start by believing in what you see Him doing. Watch for God's answers to your prayers, for His interaction in your life and in your kids' lives. Your baby spikes an unexpected fever; you pray for God's healing and the fever dissipates. You find yourself with more month than money; somehow through prayer and God's provision the bills get paid. The pastor's sermon highlights a solution for a problem that's been nagging at you for weeks. All of these incidents can be faith boosters if you see God's hand at work in them.

Your faith grows, too, when you see things you've hoped for happen. Peter illustrates this principle in the fishing incident. Though he had fished unsuccessfully all night long, he hoped something good would happen when he plopped himself back into the boat and sat at the spot where Jesus told him to fish. What a boost to Peter's faith when his boat was filled with fish. When you connect your hopes to God through prayer and Bible study, you'll find a faith boost, too.

Hoping for those unseen things—a closer walk with Him, an improved relationship with an estranged family member, godly friends for your kids, college or career guidance for your teens—will one day be as easy as plopping down on a kitchen chair or trawling for a boatload of fish. Just have faith, like Peter.

I Will

Consider how much faith I already have in God. _yes_ _no_

Examine what it means to rely on God for everything I do or need. _yes_ _no_

Look for ways to increase my faith by hoping in God for unseen things, too. _yes_ _no_

Expand my faith by sensing God's hand at work in my family and relationships. _yes_ _no_

Know that growing in faith will take time. _yes_ _no_

Ask God to show me my progress in my journey of faith. _yes_ _no_

Things to Do

 Compare the word "faith" in a regular dictionary and a Bible dictionary to catch God's viewpoint.

Write Hebrews 11:6 on a card. Post it where you see it often as a faith reminder.

Interview a mentor mom to learn her faith secrets.

Search a Bible storybook with your kids to find Bible characters who had great faith.

Take a break at lunchtime to ask God for added faith during your busy day.

Lead your kids blindfolded through the house. Talk about having faith in God for unseen things.

For a faith boost, read Hebrews 11:9–12. List three things Abraham and you have done by faith.

Things to Remember

Without faith it is impossible to please God, because anyone who comes to him must believe that he exists and that he rewards those who earnestly seek him.

HEBREWS 11:6 NIV

Abram believed the LORD and the LORD accepted Abram's faith, and that faith made him right with God.

GENESIS 15:6 NCV

> *God's power protects you through your faith until salvation is shown to you at the end of time.*
> 1 Peter 1:6 NCV

Someone might say, "You have faith, but I have deeds." Show me your faith without doing anything, and I will show you my faith by what I do.

JAMES 2:18 NCV

Jesus turned around, and when He saw her He said, "Be of good cheer, daughter; your faith has made you well." And the woman was made well from that hour.

MATTHEW 9:22 NKJV

Now faith is the substance of things hoped for, the evidence of things not seen.

HEBREWS 11:1 NKJV

Faith comes from hearing the message, and the message is heard through the word of Christ.

ROMANS 10:17 NIV

By faith we understand that the worlds were framed by the word of God, so that the things which are seen were not made of things which are visible.

HEBREWS 11:3 NKJV

Let us look only to Jesus, the One who began our faith and who makes it perfect.

HEBREWS 12:2 NCV

Since we have been made right in God's sight by faith, we have peace with God because of what Jesus Christ our Lord has done for us.

ROMANS 5:1 NLT

The purity of your faith will bring you praise and glory and honor when Jesus Christ is shown to you.

1 PETER 1:7 NCV

By grace you have been saved through faith, and that not of yourselves; it is the gift of God, not of works, lest anyone should boast.

EPHESIANS 2:8–9 NKJV

Little faith will bring your souls to Heaven, but great faith will bring Heaven to your souls.

—CHARLES H. SPURGEON

Faith makes the uplook good, the outlook bright, the inlook favorable, and the future glorious.

—DR. V. RAYMOND EDMAN

Children and Church
The Fourth Leg

Don't make your children angry by the way you treat them.
Rather, bring them up with the discipline and instruction
approved by the Lord.   —EPHESIANS 6:4 NLT

Kids are a lot like chairs—each one needs four legs to be stable and complete. Luke 2:52 says the four legs needed for a child's development are *wisdom* (knowledge and learning), *stature* (physical growth), *favor with God* (a personal faith and relationship), and *favor with men* (good friendships with others). Many times parents work hard in three of these areas, making sure their children are successful in school, healthy and up-to-date on all their shots, and surrounded by good friends. However the fourth leg—a child's spiritual life—is sometimes neglected. Just as a four-legged chair with one leg missing is wobbly and unstable, so a child without the stability of faith in God will wobble through life with an incomplete character.

To help your child develop the fourth leg of faith, make church attendance a priority. If you have been praying together at mealtime, reading stories about Jesus, or talking to your kids about God, exposing them to regular church services will reinforce the lessons you've started at home. However, don't attend church unarmed. Make your attendance meaningful by planning ahead. If your children will be sitting with you for church, remember that kids from two to ten can be active participants in much of the service.

For sermon time only, provide a small cloth bag with quiet toys—coloring or activity books; stickers, stencils, and stamps and plain white paper; brand new crayons that have sharp points; sliding number tray puzzles; tiny cars or dolls; small zipper baggies of Cheerios. Avoid anything with small parts that could fall to the floor. Keep your wiggle-worms separated, too—proximity encourages misbehavior.

Most churches also provide classes to teach children about God and His Word. Ask other moms which classes or church activities their kids enjoy. Young children might benefit from a junior church program. Middle schoolers might prefer competitions that stress Bible memorization. Your teen might be interested in membership classes or in a youth group with a community outreach. Some churches offer music opportunities for kids, too. Involving your children in any of these activities will not only strengthen their faith in God, but also help them learn to behave better and work in larger group settings.

Begin now. Strengthen the fourth leg of your kids' development by attending church services and activities regularly. Let their characters be shaped and molded by instruction from and interaction with other believers. You'll find their faith in God will grow and become an integral part of their lives, too.

I Will

Evaluate my child's development in wisdom, stature, and favor with God and others.

yes _____ *no* _____

Actively look for ways to develop my child's faith in God.

yes _____ *no* _____

Make church a priority for my family and myself.

yes _____ *no* _____

Consider how to reinforce the faith lessons learned at home and in church.

yes _____ *no* _____

Helm my kids become more involved in our church's ministry and services.

yes _____ *no* _____

Remember that church involvement and interaction can benefit m child's faith and character.

yes _____ *no* _____

Things to Do

☐ *With your kids, list the names of churches in your neighborhood. Pray for their pastors.*

☐ *To help your kids feel connected to church, research together how your church got started.*

☐ *As a family attend three different churches. Compare their worship styles with your church's style.*

☐ *Paint a poster with your kids, illustrating different things about your church: choir, building, pulpit.*

☐ *Hold a car wash or bake sale to earn money for a special church ministry.*

☐ *Call your church office. Volunteer your family's help to fold bulletins, cut grass, straighten books.*

Things to Remember

Joshua said to the people . . . "You must choose for yourselves today whom you will serve . . . As for me and my family, we will serve the LORD."

JOSHUA 24:14–15 NCV

I call to remembrance the genuine faith that is in you, which dwelt first in your grandmother Lois and your mother Eunice, and I am persuaded is in you also.

2 TIMOTHY 1:5 NKJV

I have leaned on you since the day I was born; you have been my God since my mother gave me birth.

PSALM 22:10 NCV

Only the living can praise you as I do today. Each generation can make known your faithfulness to the next.

ISAIAH 38:19 NLT

One generation shall praise Your works to another, and shall declare Your mighty acts.

PSALM 145:4 NKJV

Tell your children about it, let your children tell their children, and their children another generation.

JOEL 1:3 NKJV

The overwhelming majority in our churches today were converted before twenty-one years of age. Whatever your church does, let it do its full duty by the children.

—R. A. TORREY

A boy brought up in Sunday school is seldom brought up in court.

—DR. CLAY RISLEY

Perspective

Expand Your Vision

Look at it this way. —MATTHEW 18:12 THE MESSAGE

A newborn's cry sounds like a fire siren to a new mom, yet a more seasoned mother will chuckle and comment on how quiet that newborn's cry is. Veteran moms with toddlers know you haven't heard anything until you've heard the wail of a two-year-old who has been forced to share a favorite toy with a sibling. Those experienced moms have perspective when it comes to weeping and wailing.

Perspective—one's viewpoint of facts, ideas, or situations—colors everything you do, say, and think. Perspective determines whether you consider a glass half full or half empty. Your perspective on life also depends on your relationship to God. When life takes an unexpected turn, nonbelievers often respond to those times with complaints and grumbling. However, if you look at life from God's perspective, you can trust Him in His mercy to work everything out for your good.

And that's what God wants. He wants you to expand your vision and share His perspective. Remember what happened to Peter when he hopped out of the boat in Matthew 14:25–32?

As long as Peter kept his eyes on Jesus, he walked on top of the water. That's heavenly perspective personified—one person focusing on God no matter how rough the wind or waves. But, when Peter lost sight of Jesus, when he swapped his heavenly perspective for a worldly one, Peter began to sink. God wants you to rise above the problems in your life. So ask Him for His perspective to keep you focused on the eternal, not the immaterial.

Kids need to learn the lessons of perspective, too. Though kids live for the moment, moms know there are correlations between now and later. Model a positive perspective for your kids by exhibiting faith in them even when they fail at something. Some of your kids' most challenging experiences can become their greatest strengths later in life. Praise your kids for their determination and resourcefulness, too. These traits prove they're looking beyond obstacles to find possibilities; and looking for possibilities helps bring things into perspective.

So, if you're facing days of drudgery, piles of laundry, and wailing wee ones, stop for a moment. Look at your life from God's perspective. Recognize that your toddler will *eventually* be potty trained; your teen *will* survive driver's ed. Buried under the piles of life you'll also find slurpy kisses, silly songs, and innocent laughter. Aren't those things worth a change of perspective?

I Will

Recognize that I can choose how I view life's circumstances.

yes   *no*

Remember that I'll always have needs, but God is always there to meet them.

yes   *no*

Keep on believing that God is working out everything for my good.

yes   *no*

Stay focused on God no matter how rough the wind or waves of life.

yes   *no*

Exhibit faith in my kids—whether they succeed or fail.

yes   *no*

Actively look beyond obstacles to find possibilities and a heavenly perspective.

yes   *no*

Things to Do

☐ *Investigate Jonas Salk, who kept a positive perspective until he developed a workable polio vaccine.*

☐ *Play a virtual reality game with your kids. Discuss the difference perspective makes to the game.*

☐ *Copy Romans 8:28 onto a card. Post it to remember to view life God's way.*

☐ *Read aloud Chicken Little. Ask your kids what was wrong with Chicken Little's perspective.*

☐ *Splash through a puddle with your kids. Pretend to be Peter. Echo his perspective choices.*

☐ *Take your kids up in a hot air balloon. Discuss their view of life from that lofty level.*

Things to Remember

Look at it this way: At the right time, while we were still helpless, Christ died for ungodly people.

ROMANS 5:6 GOD'S WORD

With God's power working in us, God can do much, much more than anything we can ask or imagine.

EPHESIANS 3:20 NCV

"My thoughts are not your thoughts, neither are your ways my ways," declares the LORD. "As the heavens are higher than the earth, so are my ways higher than your ways."

ISAIAH 55:8–9 NIV

The LORD does not see as man sees; for man looks at the outward appearance, but the LORD looks at the heart.

1 SAMUEL 16:7 NKJV

The people of Israel still say, 'What the Lord does isn't fair.' People of Israel, I am fair. It is what you do that is not fair.

EZEKIEL 18:29 NCV

Who is wise? Let him understand these things. Who is prudent? Let him know them. For the ways of the LORD are right; The righteous walk in them.

HOSEA 14:9 NKJV

Wisdom is seeing life from God's perspective.

—BILL GOTHARD

When we see God, everything becomes different. It is not the external things that are different, but a different disposition looks through the same eyes as the result of the internal surgery that has taken place.

—OSWALD CHAMBERS

God's Love

A Forever Thing

I will always sing about the Lord's love.   —PSALM 89:1 NCV

Do you love your children? Some days, especially when they're terribly two or frustratingly fourteen, your love may be stretched to the limit. Even then you'd probably admit to loving your kids, for most moms love their children fiercely, absolutely. You want to give them everything that is good and protect them from sickness, accident, or disappointment. You find joy in their successes, telling everyone about their first words, first steps, or first time using the potty chair. Your heart breaks when they're sad; your anger flares when someone mistreats them. Even if your children grow up, leave home, disappoint you, and follow a path that's contrary to your lifestyle and beliefs, there will be a soft spot of love in your heart for your kids.

Yet there's someone who loves your children more than you do. That someone is God. While a mother's love is a wonderful thing, it is limited, imperfect, and will come to an end on earth when you die. God's love, however, is a forever thing. "Neither death, nor life, nor angels, nor ruling spirits, nothing now, nothing in the future, no powers, nothing above us, nothing below us, nor anything else in the whole world will ever be able to separate" you or your kids from God's love (Romans 8:38–39 NCV). All that God does for you is rooted in His love for you. Even if your kids rebel against Him and go their own way, God will still love them, too. His love never fails.

But God's love seems too good to be true. Today's television and media ads pressure moms and kids to look a certain way, wear a certain brand, or drive a certain vehicle to be accepted and loved. Some moms and kids have trouble accepting their own imperfections and therefore have trouble believing that anyone could love them with limitless love. Sometimes breakups in romantic relationships or marriages put extra barriers between moms and kids and love. Yet God doesn't love you because of the way you look, because of your personality, talents, or designer sneakers. God loves you because He made you, and you are His.

To open your hearts to God's love, moms and kids need to ignore the messages of the media and believe instead the message of the Sunday school song, "Jesus loves me; this I know. For the Bible tells me so . . ." God's love *is* a forever thing. Open your hearts . . . and believe.

I Will

Believe God loves my children and me with an unlimited, changeless love. ___ *yes* ___ *no*

Remember that God loves me because He made me. ___ *yes* ___ *no*

Know that even though I haven't always responded to God's love, He still loves me. ___ *yes* ___ *no*

Believe God loves my children more than I do. ___ *yes* ___ *no*

Ask God to forgive my shortcomings and make me more loving like He is. ___ *yes* ___ *no*

Ignore the ways the media says to find love, and look instead for God's love. ___ *yes* ___ *no*

Love my children with as much of God's love as I can. ___ *yes* ___ *no*

Things to Do

 Read Romans 8:38–39 from a children's Bible and discuss it with your children.

☐ *Use washable marker to print on your children's fingers:* G-O-D L-O-V-E-S M-E.

☐ *Discuss different kinds of love: love for cars, pets, kids. Compare these to God's love.*

☐ *Make a list of ways God has shown His love for your family. Thank Him.*

☐ *Sing a song about God's love: "Jesus Loves Me" or "Jesus Loves the Little Children."*

☐ *Make a splashy finger-paint picture to post as a reminder of God's wonderful love.*

Things to Remember

The LORD has appeared of old to me, saying: "Yes, I have loved you with an everlasting love; Therefore with loving-kindness I have drawn you."

JEREMIAH 31:3 NKJV

See how very much our heavenly Father loves us, for he allows us to be called his children, and we really are!

1 JOHN 3:1 NLT

You, O Lord, are a compassionate and gracious God, slow to anger, abounding in love and faithfulness.

PSALM 86:15 NIV

God so loved the world that He gave His only begotten Son, that whoever believes in Him should not perish but have everlasting life.

JOHN 3:16 NKJV

God shows his great love for us in this way: Christ died for us while we were still sinners.

ROMANS 5:8 NCV

The LORD is righteous in all his ways and loving toward all he has made.

PSALM 145:17 NIV

God loves you. To realize that is of paramount importance. Nothing else matters so much.

—BILLY GRAHAM

Love is God's essence, power his attribute; therefore is His love greater than his power.

—RICHARD GARNETT

Family Rules

A Fencing Lesson

Train a child in the way he should go, and when he is old he will not turn from it —PROVERBS 22:6 NIV

Children aren't born with a how-to-raise-me manual attached to their heels, but that doesn't mean families don't require an instruction manual. Families need a set of rules for the care, management, and safety of all family members. In a sense family rules are a lot like fences—they keep you out of places and from doing things you shouldn't be in or doing to begin with.

As you think about the things that are important to you in caring for your family, think in simple terms, because simple rules are effective rules. For example "Don't play in the street" is clear in its intent (and more quickly communicated as you holler it at your toddler) than saying "Honey, it's not a good idea to play in the street when you're outside today because it's very dangerous. A car could come along and drive right over you, and you and Mommy would be very, very sad." By the time you finished such a long-winded explanation your little imp could be halfway to town. Remember: simple rules are best.

Also, simple rules set in the negative will stand a chance of being remembered and followed, too. Telling a toddler "Don't ever touch the telephone" is easy to remember and will probably save you those long distance charges to Antarctica just because your toddler wanted to punch the buttons or the embarrassment of an overheard "Hi! Mommy's going potty and can't talk now." Simple rules that begin with *Don't* are sure to get your kids' attention. After all, God's Ten Commandments in Exodus 20 are all variations of "thou shalt *not*," which in modern language translates "Don't even think about it."

Remember also to keep family rules few in number: Even God had only *ten* commandments. If every action in your household has a rule attached to it, you're going to have battles erupting between you and your child every five minutes. Set rules about the important things like stealing, telling the truth, or restricting the use of dangerous objects like matches, the stove, or electrical outlets. If your children are older, you may need a family rule that reminds them to keep their hands to themselves ("Don't hit anyone." It's clear. It's enforceable.) Teenagers may need rules about the use of their after-school hours. Because of today's dress options, you might need to add something about being completely clothed before leaving the house. While "no white shoes before Memorial Day" was an important rule to your grandmother, you might want to ensure your kids are at least *wearing* shoes and clothing that covers their underwear.

To guarantee children's cooperation with family regulations, include them in the rule making process. Set aside some time for a family meeting. Announce that you will be putting together a set of family rules so that everyone from the oldest to the youngest will know what behaviors will or will not be tolerated, regardless of what the neighbor kids are allowed to do. Letting your children take part in setting up these rules will help them understand why each tenet is important. Review the rules periodically to see if changes are needed.

Once the rules are set up, you'll find your children will be glad to abide by them—for fifteen minutes or so. After that, all children at some time or another will forget or even challenge the family rules. That's where enforcement comes in; that's where a mom needs to be creative. For example, you may have discussed rules about attire during your Sunday afternoon rules-setting session. Now it's Monday morning and you've told your child it's too cold to go to school in shorts. They may protest, but a well-prepared mom will have a chart with temperatures marked off in ten-degree gradients with catalog cutouts of appropriate attire pasted alongside each number. A simple glance at the chart and a large thermometer placed beside the front door will show your scholar that 40-degree temperatures require a full complement of clothing, topped off with a coat, too.

Setting and enforcing rules is a tough task. It requires constancy and consistency. But you'll find that surrounding your home with a fence of family rules will keep things running smoothly—at least for a few minutes each day.

I Will

Accept that rules are necessary for the well-being of my family.   yes _____   no _____

Remind myself that when setting rules, simple ones are best.   yes _____   no _____

Concede that setting and enforcing rules is tough work.   yes _____   no _____

Agree to seek God's guidance as we put together workable family rules.   yes _____   no _____

Strive to be consistent in enforcing the rules we have set up.   yes _____   no _____

Things to Do

☐ To better understand God's rules, draw pictures together about one of the Ten Commandments.

☐ Read Matthew 22:34–40, noticing how many rules Jesus sets up for His disciples.

☐ God's list of rules is called the Ten Commandments. Name your list of family rules.

☐ Talk with your children about some old rules that you or your grandparents followed.

☐ Let your kids cut pictures and numbers from a catalog for your Appropriate Clothing Chart.

☐ Play a rule game. Try to think of things that do and don't have rules.

☐ Show your children how many rules are in your state's driver's manual.

Things to Remember

Children, obey your parents in all things, for this is well pleasing to the Lord.

Colossians 3:20 nkjv

Happy are those who don't listen to the wicked, who don't go where sinners go, who don't do what evil people do. They love the Lord's teachings.

Psalm 1:1–2 ncv

> Our children will hear about the wonders
> of the Lord. His righteous acts will be told
> to those yet unborn. They will hear about
> everything he has done.
> Psalm 22:30–31 nlt

Honor your father and your mother, that your days may be long upon the land which the Lord your God is giving you.

Exodus 20:12 nkjv

Whoever does not provide for relatives, and especially for family members, has denied the faith and is worse than an unbeliever.

1 Timothy 5:8 nrsv

It takes wisdom to have a good family, and it takes understanding to make it strong.

Proverbs 24:3 ncv

The rod and reproof give wisdom, but a child who gets his own way brings shame to his mother.

Proverbs 29:15 nasb

Let us pursue the things which make for peace and the things by which one may edify another.

ROMANS 14:19 NKJV

Treasure my commands within you. Keep my commands and live, and my law as the apple of your eye. Bind them on your fingers; write them on the tablet of your heart.

PROVERBS 7:1–3 NKJV

This is what you were called to do, because Christ suffered for you and gave you an example to follow. So you should do as he did.

1 PETER 2:21 NCV

My children, we should love people not only with words and talk, but by our actions and true caring.

1 JOHN 3:18 NCV

These things I want you to affirm constantly, that those who have believed in God should be careful to maintain good works. These things are good and profitable.

TITUS 3:8 NKJV

When home is ruled according to God's word, angels might be asked to stay with us, and they would not find themselves out of their element.

—CHARLES HADDON SPURGEON

The Christian home is the Master's workshop where the processes of character molding are silently, lovingly, faithfully and successfully carried on.

—RICHARD MONCKTON MILNES

Respect for Others

The Art of Manners

Never do anything that might hurt others.

—1 CORINTHIANS 10:32 NCV

It was lunchtime in the mall's crowded food court. As one family gathered around a table, fingers grabbed and hands were slapped. Voices clamored: "Give me that." "Put that down." "I want it." Diners around them frowned and hurriedly finished their meals. Tantrums happen, but this gathering evidenced a deeper problem than just a case of the grumps. Some important element was missing from this family's mealtime.

Across the food court another scene played out. A two-year-old at a crowded table loudly requested a juice-filled sipper cup: "Peese? Dink now. Peese?" Though the toddler's tone was strident, most onlookers smiled in appreciation at the youngster's demand. When the cup was delivered, diners chuckled as the little fellow muttered a slurpy-wet "Pan-ku" between swallows.

What made the difference between the two dining experiences? The magic of manners. Too often selfishness takes the place of manners, those behaviors that show respect and honor for others. Because learning to respect others is important to God and society, instruction in good manners can start early in a child's development. As your toddlers learn about colors, shapes, and animal sounds, they can also learn about courtesy and the art of saying *please* and *thank you.*

As children grow older they can learn new skills like taking turns, holding a door open for someone, or waiting for a chance to talk instead of interrupting. These behaviors will be more easily learned, too, if your child sees you using them. Good manners are effectively taught by mom's good example.

Whenever God's Word mentions good manners, the rules of respect are required of everyone, regardless of age. But sometimes adults forget to use good manners. In Luke 17:11–19, Jesus healed ten lepers of their disease. He was disappointed when only one man was well mannered enough to thank God for the miraculous healing. No one outgrows the need for good manners, and teens and adults still need to use them. Moms and older children can respect one another by courteously knocking on a closed door before entering a room, by leaving a note that says where you're going and when you'll be back, or by apologizing for rude behavior.

Good manners may not be the cure all for every family problem, but learning the art of manners can help ease some of the rough spots caused by selfishness. Manners can also help bring you and your children to a deeper relationship with God. By learning to show honor and respect for others, honoring God and respecting Him will come more easily as well.

I Will

Remember that God wants everyone to learn and use good manners.

yes _no_

Be an example of good manners for my children—in public and at home.

yes _no_

Recognize that saying _please_ and _thank you_ are important to family harmony.

yes _no_

Understand that when I use good manners I am respecting and honoring my family.

yes _no_

Look for ways to praise my children when they use good manners.

yes _no_

Things to Do

☐ Read the story in Luke 17:11–19; discuss the manners of the man who returned.

☐ Develop a family list of manners and post them where they can be seen.

☐ Teach good table manners at home, and practice these manners at a nice restaurant.

☐ Read Emilie Barnes' A Little Book of Manners _and_ A Little Book of Manners for Boys.

☐ Using good manners, role-play how to react when asked to eat something you dislike.

☐ Together write thank-you notes to someone who has done something you appreciate.

☐ Use errand time in the car to discuss how good manners can honor God.

Things to Remember

Let each of you look out not only for his own interests, but also for the interests of others.

PHILIPPIANS 2:4 NKJV

When you go out to dinner with an influential person, mind your manners: Don't gobble your food, don't talk with your mouth full. And don't stuff yourself; bridle your appetite.

PROVERBS 23:1–3 THE MESSAGE

Show respect to old people; stand up in their presence. Show respect also to your God.

LEVITICUS 19:32 NCV

Give to everyone what you owe them: Pay your taxes and import duties, and give respect and honor to all to whom it is due.

ROMANS 13:7 NLT

Show respect for all people: Love the brothers and sisters of God's family, respect God, honor the king.

1 PETER 2:17 NCV

Each of you must respect his mother and father, and you must observe my Sabbaths. I am the LORD your God.

LEVITICUS 19:3 NIV

Nothing is ever lost by courtesy. It is the cheapest of the pleasures; costs nothing and conveys much. It pleases him who gives and him who receives, and thus, like mercy, it is twice blessed.

—ERASTUS WIMAN

He that respects not is not respected.

—GEORGE HERBERT

Promises

Cross Your Heart

We can trust God to do what he promised.

—HEBREWS 10:23 NCV

"Cross your heart?" This query occurs often in kids' conversations. Kids who promise anything to other kids inevitably get asked the question "Cross your heart?" in an attempt to ascertain trustworthiness. Keeping your promise is important.

Hidden within any promise is a message of commitment, an indication of character, and an underlying connection between people. If you promise to attend a friend's wedding, you're making a commitment of your time and energy to get to that wedding; you're making a statement about your character that says you're trustworthy; and you're letting your friend know how important he or she is to you. Promises are a big deal.

Think about the promises you make. "Get your toys picked up, and we'll read a story" is a promise easily given and kept because both parties benefit—mom gets a clean room; the kids get a story. The harder promises for moms to keep are often ones made in frustration. One new mom learned this the hard way.

Her one-year-old had discovered that by holding on to the nipple of a bottle and swinging it around her head the nipple and bottle would separate, slinging the bottle's contents everywhere. Mom said "Don't do that" as she gave her daughter a new bottle. Immediately the little girl whirled the *new* bottle and it, too, smashed onto the floor. Mom was frustrated. And Mom made a rash promise: "Do that again, and you'll never get another bottle." A wicked gleam, a rebellious streak, and the next bottle of juice whirled and splashed. Now mom had a problem. She had made a promise, so she kept her word even though it meant more work for her. The toddler never got another bottle, but became a cup user that day. And the new mom learned to be careful and not make any more hasty promises.

The same lesson applies to you. If you find your kids or yourself getting tired, frustrated, or angry, be careful. Don't speak in haste, or you might make a promise you'd rather not keep. Instead, call a time out. Reflect on God's faithfulness in fulfilling His promises: to be with you, to forgive your sins, to adopt you and bless you. He promised to make Abraham into a great nation, to give David an everlasting kingdom, and to give barren Elizabeth a child. God keeps His promises. Will you keep the promises you make to your kids? Cross your heart?

I Will

Remind myself of the importance of keeping my promises.

yes _____ _no_ _____

Understand that a promise is a message of commitment to another person.

yes _____ _no_ _____

Ask God to help me keep my promises.

yes _____ _no_ _____

Remember that my promises include an unspoken message about my trustworthiness.

yes _____ _no_ _____

Be careful to avoid making promises I cannot keep.

yes _____ _no_ _____

Reflect on God's promises to me and rejoice.

yes _____ _no_ _____

Know that I can always trust God to keep His promises.

yes _____ _no_ _____

Things to Do

☐ _Tell the story of Noah to your kids. Discuss the promise God made to Noah (Genesis 9:11)._

☐ _Draw and color a rainbow. List different promises from God on each color band._

☐ _Make a promise chart. When your kids make and keep a promise, give them a star._

☐ _Attend a wedding with your kids and talk later about the promises given and received._

☐ _With your kids, write a prayer to God thanking Him for keeping His promises._

☐ _Play a promise game with your kids, listing five promises you can and cannot keep._

Things to Remember

Sarah herself also received strength to conceive seed, and she bore a child when she was past the age, because she judged Him faithful who had promised.

HEBREWS 11:11 NKJV

These two things cannot change: God cannot lie when he makes a promise, and he cannot lie when he makes an oath.

HEBREWS 6:18 NCV

God faithfully keeps his promises. He called you to be partners with his Son Jesus Christ our Lord.

1 CORINTHIANS 1:9 GOD'S WORD

If some Jews were not faithful to him, will that stop God from doing what he promised? No! God will continue to be true even when every person is false.

ROMANS 3:3–4 NCV

Through his glory and integrity he has given us his promises that are of the highest value. Through these promises you will share in the divine nature.

2 PETER 1:4 GOD'S WORD

Your kingdom is an everlasting kingdom, and your dominion endures through all generations. The LORD is faithful to all his promises and loving toward all he has made.

PSALM 145:13 NIV

It is better to run the risk of being considered indecisive, better to be uncertain and not promise, than to promise and not fulfill.

—OSWALD CHAMBERS

Wait at God's promise until He meets you there, for He always returns by the path of His promises.

—MRS. CHARLES E. COWMAN

God's Image

Like a Mother

God created human beings in his image. In the image of God he created them. —GENESIS 1:27 NCV

Do you look like your mom or dad? Do you have your great-grandma's eyes or grandpa's nose? Whether you like it or not, such physical characteristics often stamp you as one of the family. God's Word says you carry another family stamp, too. Because you have been created in God's image, you share some of His characteristics. In fact, the very gifts God has given you to raise your children are all facets of His image, all ways in which God acts like a mother, too. God is:

M—Merciful. God does not always give His children what they deserve, but rather forgives and shows mercy when they do wrong. When you show mercy to your children when they do wrong, you reflect this facet of God to your little ones.

O—Observant. God knows all and sees all. Many times children think moms have eyes in the back of their heads because moms seem to see everything. When you keep an observant eye on your kids, you're modeling another of God's characteristics.

T—Trustworthy. When you reach out your arms, tell your kids to jump, and they fly through the air into your embrace, your kids are proclaiming your trustworthiness. God is never false; He can be trusted. He's true to His word, true to His nature; you bear that image, too.

H—Helpful. God is always there, without fail, to help His children. Though you may not always be available to your kids, your willingness to give your children whatever help they need reveals this trait of God's character at work in your life.

E—Encouraging. You stand behind your kids with encouragement, motivating them to do right and reach their full potential, just like God stands with you, encouraging you to say and do the right things.

R—Righteous. God is holy, upright, good. As God's child, made in His image, bearing the mark of His honesty, goodness, and respectability, you show your children that righteousness is something to strive for.

What wonderful attributes. What fantastic facets of God's character. As a child of God made in His image, the characteristics of God listed in this acrostic are already at work in your life. They're transforming you into the mother God wants you to be. Look closely. Can you see the family resemblance?

I Will

Believe God is merciful and ask Him to help me
show mercy, too.

yes _____ _no_ _____

Trust God to give me eyes to see as He sees.

yes _____ _no_ _____

Learn from God how to be more trustworthy with my
kids and others.

yes _____ _no_ _____

Rely on God's help for everything I do.

yes _____ _no_ _____

Look to God for the encouragement I need
as a mom.

yes _____ _no_ _____

Praise God for the ways His righteousness is
reflected in me to my family.

yes _____ _no_ _____

Things to Do

☐ *Using a Bible concordance, find verses that talk about God's righteousness, strength, and mercy.*

☐ *Print GOD IS on a sheet of paper. Fill it with words that describe Him.*

☐ *Sing a song together about God's character, like "God Is So Good to Me."*

☐ *Create a rap with your children about one of God's attributes. Repeat it together.*

☐ *Have a contest. See who can find the acrostic's Bible verses the fastest.*

☐ *Pray, thanking God each day for a specific aspect of His character you appreciate.*

☐ *Draw a rainbow. Print a godly characteristic you want to demonstrate on each color band.*

Things to Remember

In Him we live and move and have our being, as also some of your own poets have said, "For we are also His offspring."

ACTS 17:28 NKJV

Like babies you will be nursed and held in my arms and bounced on my knees. I will comfort you as a mother comforts her child.

ISAIAH 66:12–13 NCV

There is no one holy like the LORD. There is no God but you; there is no Rock like our God.

1 SAMUEL 2:2 NCV

Your mercy, O LORD, is in the heavens; Your faithfulness reaches to the clouds.

PSALM 36:5 KJV

Taste and see that the LORD is good; blessed is the man who takes refuge in him.

PSALM 34:8 NIV

He does not become tired or need to rest. No one can understand how great his wisdom is.

ISAIAH 40:28 NCV

Persons of true godly character are neither optimists nor pessimists, but realists who have confidence in God.

—WARREN WIERSBE

In the maddening maze of things, and tossed by storm and flood, to one fixed trust my spirit clings: I know that God is good.

—JOHN GREENLEAF WHITTIER

Bible Study

Shovel While It's Snowing

Things were written in the Scriptures long ago to teach us. They give us hope and encouragement. —ROMANS 15:4 NLT

God's Word is a living letter of love. Written by many people under the direction of God's Holy Spirit, every page in your Bible fits together to bring God's message to His children everywhere. God's Word tells of His love for you and His gifts of joy and peace. God's Word offers you a wealth of wisdom and a way to stay connected to Him despite distance, time, or situation.

Since God's Word is full of wonderful things, why don't moms spend more time in Bible study? One major reason: kids. Children are experts at Bible study sabotage, whether they mean to be or not. You plop down in a chair, pick up God's Word, start to read, and the baby begins to cry. Later you decide to read a passage of God's Word aloud to your child and learn something together. This time you're interrupted by a wiggly worm who needs to go potty. Your Bible ends up on the coffee table or nightstand buried under the mail or a layer of dust before you pick it up again. Trying to study God's Word with little ones in the house seems as futile as shoveling the sidewalk while it's still snowing.

Northerners know that even though it might seem futile to shovel snow while it's still snowing, the exercise actually makes sense. Each shovel of the white stuff you move now means one less shovel full you'll need to move later on. Bible study follows a similar principle. Every little piece you can work into your schedule now will result in a closer walk with God, both now and later on, too. Here's how to make it work.

Some moms are like day lilies—as soon as the sun comes up, they're raring to go. Other moms are night owls—their minds don't begin to function until suppertime. Work with your body's preference and start small. Daytime or nighttime, it doesn't matter, just set aside fifteen minutes to claim as your Bible study time. Make sure everything is ready in advance— your Bible, a pen, some clean paper or a journal. (Don't use your fifteen minutes to locate supplies.) Begin with a quick prayer, asking God to show Himself to you as you study. Then read God's Word as a living letter addressed to you.

Start with the easy stuff. Try a chapter of Proverbs, matching the chapter number to the date on the calendar. Continue with one chapter from one of the shorter books in the New Testament. (If you need joy, start with Philippians. If you want some daily how-to's, try Colossians.) Using your pen and paper, answer two questions: *What does this passage tell me about God? What does this passage say about me?* With the moments you have left, copy down one verse that stands out or means something to you in the chapters you've just read. Put this verse where you can glance at it often until your next

Bible study time—on the refrigerator, by the kitchen sink, on the sun visor of your car. Then finish your study time with a quick prayer of thanks.

Don't be upset at yourself if you miss a day or two. God understands. Just try again. Researchers know that it takes two weeks to form bad habits; good habits take longer. As you find more time, dig deeper during your Bible study. Check out what God says about setting priorities, raising children, rekindling your marriage. Look up all the mothers in the Bible and learn from their experiences. Memorize portions of Scripture so that you can recall God's words to you when you're driving down the freeway or sitting up all night with a colicky baby.

One day your family will see your consistency at Bible study and comment on it. Since a part of being a mom is sharing your love of God's Word with your children, ask them to participate in Bible study with you. If they can read and write, give them a Bible storybook. Let them write down what they learn about God, too. Compare notes occasionally, if you like. Remember, God's Word is His living letter to you. Take some time to read your "mail" today and share God's letter with your kids, too.

I Will

Acknowledge that God's Word should be more than a coffee table centerpiece in my home.

<u>yes</u>   <u>no</u>

Know that God's truths are hidden within the pages of His living letter to me.

<u>yes</u>   <u>no</u>

Assume that finding time for Bible study will not be easy, but will be worthwhile.

<u>yes</u>   <u>no</u>

Pray for understanding as I read and learn from God's Word.

<u>yes</u>   <u>no</u>

Recognize that when I miss Bible study for a day, I need to start again.

<u>yes</u>   <u>no</u>

Things to Do

☐ *Invest some time and money in finding a good study Bible.*

☐ *Send a letter to your child. Explain how God's Word is a letter, too.*

☐ *Ask your church if they offer a Bible study that fits your schedule, and sign up.*

☐ *Put your special Bible verses in a box labeled PEARLS. Read them for a pick-me-up.*

☐ *List four things 2 Timothy 3:16–17 says about Bible study.*

☐ *Read a Bible storybook to your children at bedtime. Ask what they learned about God.*

☐ *Weave ribbon bookmarks for your kids as reminders to weave God's Word into life through Bible study.*

Things to Remember

How sweet are Your words to my taste, sweeter than honey to my mouth! Through Your precepts I get understanding; therefore I hate every false way.

PSALM 119:103–104 NKJV

God's word is alive and working and is sharper than a double-edged sword. It cuts all the way into us, where the soul and the spirit are joined.

HEBREWS 4:12 NCV

Let us discern for ourselves what is right; let us learn together what is good.
Job 34:4 NIV

Your testimonies I have taken as a heritage forever, for they are the rejoicing of my heart. I have inclined my heart to perform Your statutes forever.

PSALM 119:111–112 NKJV

You will have minds confident and at rest, focused on Christ, God's great mystery. All the richest treasures of wisdom and knowledge are embedded in that mystery and nowhere else.

COLOSSIANS 2:2–3 THE MESSAGE

Oh, how I love Your law! It is my meditation all the day.

PSALM 119:97 NKJV

Grow in the grace and knowledge of our Lord and Savior Jesus Christ.

2 PETER 3:18 NASB

The teachings of the LORD are perfect; they give new strength. The rules of the LORD can be trusted; they make plain people wise.

PSALM 19:7 NCV

Your testimonies are wonderful; therefore my soul keeps them. The entrance of Your words gives light; it gives understanding to the simple.

PSALM 119:129–130 NKJV

Continue following the teachings you learned. You know they are true, because you trust those who taught you. Since you were a child you have known the Holy Scriptures.

2 TIMOTHY 3:14–15 NCV

He must always keep this copy of the law with him and read it daily as long as he lives. That way he will learn to fear the LORD.

DEUTERONOMY 17:19 NLT

I do not turn aside from Your law. I remembered Your judgments of old, O LORD, and have comforted myself.

PSALM 119:51–52 NKJV

Bible study is like eating peanuts. The more you eat, the more you want to eat.

—PAUL LITTLE

The Bible is God's chart for you to steer by, to keep you from the bottom of the sea, and to show you where the harbor is.

—HENRY WARD BEECHER

Sibling Rivalry

Infernal Fraternal Fracases

Avoiding quarrels will bring you honor. —PROVERBS 20:3 NCV

It's a fact of life. The only way to avoid sibling conflict is to have only one child. Two or more children in any family unlock the potential for sibling squabbles. Your children's ages, personalities, and reasons for fighting, however, should determine how you react to sibling rivalry.

Very young children have difficulty sharing. To prevent fights before they start, let your children set aside three or four special toys that do not have to be shared with anyone else. Put these items aside in a special place. Let each child know that everything else must be shared without a fuss. When fights *do* break out, let young children work out their aggressions by washing a sliding glass or storm door. Give each child a paper towel moistened with glass cleaner. Station them on either side of the door with instructions to clean their side of the glass. Before the glass is clean, the kids might be laughing.

Remember that children fight more often when they're bored, tired, or hungry. Listen to their voices to see if your children are getting aggressive. If boredom's the reason, suggest new activities to distract them from fighting. Send tired children to bed for a nap or to separate chairs to watch a video. Hungry children often fight over food, too, so institute a divide-or-choose policy. One child divides the last piece of anything into two servings; the other child has first choice of which serving they want. This two-child process ensures that the divider will keep things more equal.

As your children grow up, tactics for solving sibling fracases change. Children need to learn how to settle disagreements by themselves. Moms may referee by setting limits to fights—no physical abuse allowed—and by clearly communicating that disagreements need to be resolved. One mom uses this reminder: "Either you settle this nicely, or I'll settle it for you. And you won't be happy if I do." Also, declare a neutral zone for all parties—a place where each child can escape the fight. When combatants retreat to this zone, others cannot follow them there—physically or verbally.

Unfortunately moms can sometimes be the cause of those infernal fights. Spending more time with one child on homework can be perceived as unfair to another. A mom's verbal comparisons of her children can build resentment between siblings. So be fair. Be sensitive. Dealing with sibling rivalry is hard enough. Don't put yourself in the middle of the mix, too.

I Will

Place a high value on each member of my family. _yes_ _no_

Recognize that sibling fights are a part of life. _yes_ _no_

Acknowledge that I can head off sibling conflicts by keeping my kids from getting overtired. _yes_ _no_

Consider that my best intentions toward one child may be perceived as unfairness to another. _yes_ _no_

Trust God to help me be fair, sensitive, and loving with my kids. _yes_ _no_

Accept that squabbling and making up is part of learning to settle disagreements. _yes_ _no_

Things to Do

☐ *Read Genesis 13 and discuss how Abram avoided a fight with his nephew Lot.*

☐ *Separate quarreling children to opposite sides of the room. Give each an activity to do.*

☐ *Offer older children an option: Settle your dispute or you'll be given a distasteful chore.*

☐ *Let angry children sing their complaints and concerns at each other.*

☐ *Suggest an alternative to a fight. Try: "Don't fight, and we'll read two stories tonight."*

☐ *To end a fight, require each child to tell the other five nice compliments.*

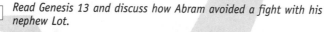

Things to Remember

The beginning of strife is like letting out water, so abandon the quarrel before it breaks out.

PROVERBS 17:14 NASB

I appeal to you by the authority of the Lord Jesus Christ to stop arguing among yourselves. Let there be real harmony so there won't be divisions in the church.

1 CORINTHIANS 1:10 NLT

Pride only breeds quarrels, but wisdom is found in those who take advice.

PROVERBS 13:10 NIV

You are joined together with peace through the Spirit, so make every effort to continue together in this way.

EPHESIANS 4:3 NCV

Fools quickly show that they are upset, but the wise ignore insults.

PROVERBS 12:16 NCV

Don't let evil get the best of you; get the best of evil by doing good.

ROMANS 12:20 THE MESSAGE

There is no winning or losing in a good conflict, but a breaking through to better understanding of each other.

—CAROLE MAYHALL

When we train ourselves to attack our problems rather than people, we work our way toward healthy resolution without leaving casualties in our wake.

—ELISA MORGAN

Remembering

A Stack of Stones

Remember the Lord, who is great and powerful.

—NEHEMIAH 4:14 NCV

In a children's card game, identical pairs of animal photos are shuffled and randomly dealt facedown. Children take turns peeking under two cards at a time, revealing the photo of the animal for a brief moment. The object of the game is to locate the matching pairs of animals by remembering where you've seen each one. But sometimes your mind plays tricks. You think you've seen the elephant in one spot, only to peek under that card and find it's a lion. Remembering is harder than it looks.

The folks who manufacture calendars, handheld planners, and watches with built-in alarms recognize how tough remembering all you have to remember can be. Some things you'd rather forget, like income taxes or hurt feelings, but remembering can keep you safe (if you remember the traffic laws), your tummy full (if you remember to cook supper), and your family happy (if you remember Aunt Susie's birthday is *tomorrow*).

Remembering is important to God, too. When the Israelites crossed the Jordan River into the Promised Land,

God instructed Joshua and the leaders of Israel to pick up stones from the river and pile them up. These stones were to remind the Israelites of God's blessings. When children in subsequent generations asked their parents why a pile of stones stood beside the river, these stones of remembrance could remind later generations of God's goodness, too.

How do you remember things? Do you take photographs or videos of your kids? Do you keep a journal of each week's happenings? Do you carry a planner? One mom refers to her kitchen calendar as her brain because it's full of birthday and anniversary information, changes of address, telephone numbers, notes about sermons, prayer requests and answers. That's major remembering.

More importantly, do you and your kids remember God and His kindnesses? Why not use Joshua's example and build some stones of remembrance into your family life. Compare notes together while trapped in the car going to an appointment. Remember ways that God has answered a prayer, provided a need, taken special care of you. As you turn over the memories of God's kindnesses, assign a visible token to each of these moments—a colorful pebble or seashell, a window cling, photograph, or a strand of embroidery thread. Remembering is harder than it looks, so surround yourself with whatever it takes to be reminded. And then, when your children and grandchildren ask about your unusual collection, remember God's goodness together.

I Will

Acknowledge that remembering isn't an easy thing to do.

yes *no*

Understand that God wants my children and me to remember Him always.

yes *no*

Actively seek ways to surround myself with reminders of God's kindness.

yes *no*

Choose to remember only the good things, forgiving and forgetting the bad.

yes *no*

Share with others the ways God has blessed my family and me.

yes *no*

Find ways to help my children remember God's active participation in their lives.

yes *no*

Things to Do

☐ *Play the memory card game with your kids. Use any cards that have matching pairs.*

☐ *Memorize a Bible verse that begins with the first letter of your child's name.*

☐ *Read and discuss the story of Joshua's remembrance stones with your kids (Joshua 13:14–14:22).*

☐ *Plant a remembrance garden. Let each plant remind you of a friend or family member.*

☐ *Ask your kids to talk about their earliest remembrances. Share what you remember, too.*

☐ *Praise your kids for remembering three things (be specific). Forget to remind them of their forgetfulness.*

Things to Remember

I will remember the works of the LORD; surely I will remember Your wonders of old.

PSALM 77:11 NKJV

Be very careful never to forget what you have seen the LORD do for you . . . And be sure to pass them on to your children and grandchildren.

DEUTERONOMY 4:9 NLT

Each generation can set its hope anew on God, remembering his glorious miracles and obeying his commands.

PSALM 78:7 NLT

You shall remember the LORD your God, for it is He who gives you power to get wealth.

DEUTERONOMY 8:18 NKJV

Bless the LORD, O my soul, and all that is within me, bless His holy name. Bless the LORD, O my soul, and forget none of His benefits.

PSALM 103:1–2 NASB

All the ends of the earth will remember and turn to the LORD, and all the families of the nations will worship before You. For the kingdom is the LORD's and He rules over the nations.

PSALM 22:27–28 NASB

He who receives a good turn should never forget it; he who does one should never remember it.

—PIERRE CHARRON

Remember the wonderful blessings that come to you each day from the hands of a generous and gracious God, and forget the irritations that would detract from your happiness.

—WILLIAM ARTHUR WARD

Forgiveness

Skinned Knees and Elbows

Forgive us our debts, as we forgive our debtors.

—MATTHEW 6:12 NKJV

Skinned knees and elbows are a part of growing up, but the total healing process takes time. The bleeding has to stop; a scab has to form; and a scar has to materialize. Sometimes kids pick at the scabs, making the wounds bleed again. Moms know the best way to heal a skinned knee or elbow is to clean it, cover it, and leave it alone.

Forgiveness works along those same principles. When someone says or does something mean or unkind to you or your kids, those hurtful acts wound your heart. Holding on to those hurts, nursing a grudge, or allowing the hurt to grow into bitterness only encourages the wound to bleed more. Picking the injury apart every time you see the one who hurt you stops the healing process, too, just like picking at scabs keeps skinned knees from healing. God's Word says the only way to heal a heart that has been injured is to cleanse and cover the hurt with forgiveness and then forget that the injury ever took place.

That's what God does. Whenever you sin or choose to do things your way instead of God's way, the bond between you and God is severed. But Micah 7:18 assures you there is a way for you to reconnect to God—forgiveness. God is always willing to forgive. His forgiveness is so vast, so wonderful, He "will throw away all our sins into the deepest part of the sea" (Micah 7:19 NCV). God not only forgives your sins, He forgets them, too. He doesn't hold a grudge or keep a list of your wrongdoings. He chooses to see your sin, wash it with your apology, cleanse it with His "I forgive you," and then leave the hurt alone, turning His back on it so that the break in your relationship can be mended. In fact, God's forgetfulness of your forgiven sins is so great, God's Word says He doesn't remember what caused the heartbreak to begin with.

What an example for you to follow when it comes to forgiving your kids or showing them how to forgive others. Sometimes it seems easier to overlook bad behavior, to act as if something wrong never happened, or to make an excuse for the unkind person because they were tired, overworked, or stressed. Responding to situations in these ways only buries the hurts and hard feelings. Just as wounds need to be cleansed in order to heal, so hurts have to be acknowledged for hearts to heal, too.

When hurts happen in your family, follow these suggestions. If you have quarreled with your children about something, whether you are right or wrong, you probably said more than you meant to say. Don't let the argument fester. Make up with your kids quickly. Don't make them come to you, either, begging for your forgiveness. Since you are the adult, be the first one to cleanse wounded hearts by apologizing for the hurtful words you said. When you ask for your child's forgiveness, tell them why you got so mad at them, why you said what you said. Your explanation makes it easier for your kids to forgive you and to steer clear of repeating those behaviors again.

While unkindness or meanness can be forgiven, children also need to learn there are consequences to hurtful actions. When the Israelites refused to trust God and conquer the Promised Land, God forgave them for their doubt, but refused to let that generation of faithless Israelites enter the land at all. Every Israelite who refused to trust God died while wandering through the Sinai Desert. In the same way, if a child willfully breaks something or does something mean, some punishment that fits the crime is appropriate. Discuss the options together. Your child might write a letter asking for forgiveness, apologize in person, receive a spanking or time out, pay for something broken, or a combination of options.

Just as skinned knees and elbows can heal and be restored as good as new, so relationships can be made as good as new, too, through the gift of forgiveness. God offers you that wonderful gift every day. Accept it, and then pass it along to others so that you can enjoy the blessing of relationships healed through forgiveness.

I Will

Know that my children and I need forgiveness
every day.   yes   no

Thank God for His wonderful, immeasurable gift
of forgiveness.   yes   no

Try to follow God's example and forget the wrongs
that have been done to me.   yes   no

Choose to remember the forgiveness others have
shown my children and me.   yes   no

Refuse to carry the burden of resentment and
bitterness over past hurts and wrongs.   yes   no

Things to Do

- [ ] *Write a note to say thank you to someone who has forgiven you.*

- [ ] *Draw a cartoon panel illustrating Joseph's forgiveness of his brothers in Genesis 50:15–21.*

- [ ] *Write Psalm 32:1 on paper. Wrap it like a present, remembering forgiveness is God's gift.*

- [ ] *Read 2 Samuel 12:1–14 with your kids. Discuss David's sin, consequences, and forgiveness.*

- [ ] *Ask children if people should be forgiven, punished, or both for lying, vandalism, or speeding.*

- [ ] *Make I-forgive-you placemats. Let your kids use them at mealtime as forgiveness reminders.*

- [ ] *List three bad things your kids have done. Ask God's forgiveness. Throw the list away.*

Things to Remember

In Him we have redemption through His blood, the forgiveness of sins, according to the riches of His grace.

EPHESIANS 1:7 NKJV

You have forgiven the iniquity of Your people; you have covered all their sin.

PSALM 85:2 NKJV

Put up with each other, and forgive each other if anyone has a complaint. Forgive as the Lord forgave you.
Colossians 3:13 GOD'S WORD

They should stop their evil thoughts. They should return to the LORD so he may have mercy on them. They should come to our God, because he will freely forgive them.

ISAIAH 55:7 NCV

If My people who are called by My name will humble themselves, and pray and seek My face . . . then I will hear from heaven, and will forgive their sin.

2 CHRONICLES 7:14 NKJV

You are forgiving and good, O Lord, abounding in love to all who call to you.

PSALM 86:5 NIV

Whenever you stand praying, forgive, if you have anything against anyone, so that your Father who is in heaven will also forgive you your transgressions.

MARK 11:25 NASB

I will forgive them for the wicked things they did, and I will not remember their sins anymore.

HEBREWS 8:12 NCV

I, I am the One who forgives all your sins, for my sake; I will not remember your sins.

ISAIAH 43:25 NCV

If we confess our sins, He is faithful and just to forgive us our sins and to cleanse us from all unrighteousness.

1 JOHN 1:9 KJV

"Let's discuss this!" says the LORD. "Though your sins are bright red, they will become as white as snow. Though they are dark red, they will become as white as wool."

ISAIAH 1:18 GOD'S WORD

I tell you the truth, all sins that people do and all the things people say against God can be forgiven.

MARK 3:28 NCV

"I can forgive but I cannot forget" is only another way of saying "I cannot forgive."

—HENRY WARD BEECHER

When God forgives He forgets. He buries our sins in the sea and puts a sign on the bank saying, "No Fishing Allowed."

—CORRIE TEN BOOM

God Uses You

Just Ordinary People

Always give yourselves fully to the work of the Lord.
—1 CORINTHIANS 15:58 NIV

As you study God's Word you'll discover an amazing fact. Since the beginning of time, God has used ordinary people to do extraordinary things for Him. All those familiar Bible characters whose stories you've heard from childhood—Noah, Abraham, Joseph, Moses, Samson, Ruth, Esther, Daniel, Jonah, David, Peter, and Paul—were imperfect, flawed, ordinary people. But God chose to use them to further His kingdom and fulfill His plan. Their lives illustrate that moms don't have to be perfect or special in any way to be used by God; moms just have to be committed to Him.

Perhaps you think of yourself as an ordinary mother with no special gifts or abilities. You do your best on a daily basis to raise your children the way you think God wants you to, but you know you don't always accomplish your goals. Sometimes you get angry. Well, Moses had a bad temper, too. Sometimes you're impatient with your children. Remember, Abraham got so impatient with God, he fathered a child with his wife's maid. That caused all kinds of problems. Sometimes you might feel you just can't do what God wants you to do, so you turn your back on what you know is God's will. So did Jonah. He turned around and ran the opposite way when he found out what God wanted him to do.

See? You're not that different from all those giants of the faith you read about in God's Word. They didn't have super strengths or abilities. In fact, it was their weakness that allowed God to use them. First Corinthians 1:27 reminds moms that "God chose the foolish things of the world to shame the wise, and he chose the weak things of the world to shame the strong" (NCV). When you sense your own inability to do something God wants you to do, but trust God to do it anyway, that's when He can use you to further His kingdom and bring Him greater glory.

God uses mothers in very special ways, too. You're His representative to share His love with your children. God wants to use you to help them understand the important principles of kindness, goodness, and faith. Studies have shown that the most influential person in a child's life is his or her mother. Let God use you to draw your children *to* Him and to teach them how to live *for* Him. It's the greatest work you'll ever do.

I Will

Admit my weaknesses to God.   _yes_ ____   _no_ ____

Commit myself each day to God and ask Him to use me as He pleases.   _yes_ ____   _no_ ____

Realize that my strengths may not be what God will use to glorify Himself.   _yes_ ____   _no_ ____

Love my children with God's strong love.   _yes_ ____   _no_ ____

Recognize that God has a plan for me and my children.   _yes_ ____   _no_ ____

Be aware of how God uses other people in my life.   _yes_ ____   _no_ ____

Believe that God can use me to do extraordinary things.   _yes_ ____   _no_ ____

Things to Do

☐ _Learn about Peter in John's Gospel to see how God used an ordinary person._

☐ _Write a poem or rap with your children about how God can use you._

☐ _Discuss with your children the idea that little is much when God is in it._

☐ _Ask some Christian friends how God has used them in surprising ways._

☐ _Read Romans 12:1–2 to find out how to be of best use to God._

☐ _List ways you feel God has already used you. Thank God for them._

☐ _Write down five things about God you'd like to teach your children this year._

Things to Remember

To each one is given the manifestation of the Spirit for the common good.

1 CORINTHIANS 12:7 NASB

All who make themselves clean from evil will be used for special purposes. They will be made holy, useful to the Master, ready to do any good work.

2 TIMOTHY 2:21 NCV

Prepare your minds for action; be self-controlled; set your hope fully on the grace to be given you when Jesus Christ is revealed.

1 PETER 1:13 NIV

He brings us alongside someone else who is going through hard times so that we can be there for that person just as God was there for us.

2 CORINTHIANS 1:4 THE MESSAGE

In the same way, you should be a light for other people. Live so that they will see the good things you do and will praise your Father in heaven.

MATTHEW 5:16 NCV

Only fear the LORD, and serve Him in truth with all your heart; for consider what great things He has done for you.

1 SAMUEL 12:24 NKJV

Is your place a small place? Tend it with care!—He set you there. Whate'er your place, it is not yours alone, but His who set you there.

—JOHN OXENHAM

I used to ask God to help me. Then I asked if I might help Him. I ended up by asking Him to do His work through me.

—JAMES HUDSON TAYLOR

Discipline

Plenty Good

This teaching is a light, and the corrections of discipline are the way to life. —PROVERBS 6:23 NIV

Try this experiment. Walk through an average day in your family's life from the pint-size perspective of your youngest child. Look and listen to everything. With those images in mind, you can more carefully consider mothering's greatest challenges—discipline. All children need to know what is expected of them, and every family needs to set boundaries or family rules that define these expectations. Discipline revolves around these defined boundaries; when a line is crossed, action of some kind—discipline, correction, reproof—is required. In fact, God's Word says that "a refusal to correct is a refusal to love; [so] love your children by disciplining them" (Proverbs 13:24 THE MESSAGE).

Yet discipline shouldn't come from an angry heart or heavy hand. Research indicates that the more positive you can be in administering discipline, the less rebellion you'll have when your terrible two matures into a fearsome fourteen. Even three-year-olds can be held accountable for their actions, so try to praise the good and ignore most of the bad, unless it is overtly disobedient or willful. Urge kindness and respect for all family members, too. Let positive words frame the orders you give your kids. For example, instead of saying, "You need to get ready for bed" try "If you're in pj's in five minutes, we'll read your favorite book."

However, just as generals give orders to their troops, moms often have to issue orders, too. Most of these orders are simple requests—brush your teeth; let the cat out; put your dishes in the sink. But there are times when orders are more important to personal safety—put that knife down; don't run into the street; buckle your seat belt. Whenever you issue such orders, be prepared to immediately enforce them. Give your children a chance to obey by letting them know you will give them to the count of three to carry out your orders. But, if you get to the number three and your child hasn't complied, a restriction of privileges, a stint in the time-out chair, or some such punishment is in order. Refuse to acknowledge any tantrums, but congratulate your kids for prompt obedience, especially if you want good behavior repeated.

Finally, prove your love to your kids with the plenty-good approach to discipline: supply *plenty* of rest for cranky kids, *plenty* of love all the time, and *plenty* of praise for good conduct to ensure *good* attitudes, *good* behavior, and a *good* family atmosphere. That sounds plenty good.

I Will

Understand the importance of setting clear family boundaries. _____ yes _____ no

Acknowledge that loving my kids means disciplining them when necessary. _____ yes _____ no

Make sure the discipline I administer doesn't come with a heavy hand or angry heart. _____ yes _____ no

Urge kindness and respect be shown for all family members to reduce discipline problems. _____ yes _____ no

Remember that my kids can and should be held accountable for their actions. _____ yes _____ no

Look for positive ways to word the simple requests I make of my kids. _____ yes _____ no

Things to Do

☐ *Discuss discipline issues with your child's teacher even if things are going well.*

☐ *Devise a family signal—hand clap, whistle, finger snap—to say instant obedience is needed to avoid danger.*

☐ *Read 2 Samuel 13. Journal your impressions of David's lack of discipline with his sons.*

☐ *Set aside a time-out chair for discipline problems. A child's age can be the time-out time limit.*

☐ *Analyze the discipline you give one day this week. List ways to be more positive in the future.*

☐ *Make a goodness chart. Give stickers for good behavior, doing chores, brushing teeth.*

Things to Remember

Why do you call Me "Lord, Lord," and not do the things which I say?

LUKE 6:46 NKJV

This is love: that we walk in obedience to his commands. As you have heard from the beginning, his command is that you walk in love.

2 JOHN 1:6 NIV

Happy are those who keep his rules, who try to obey him with their whole heart.

PSALM 119:2 NCV

Even more blessed are all who hear the word of God and put it into practice.

LUKE 11:28 NLT

Do what God's word says. Don't merely listen to it, or you will fool yourselves.

JAMES 1:22 GOD'S WORD

I thought about my ways, and turned my feet to Your testimonies. I made haste, and did not delay to keep Your commandments.

PSALM 119:59–60 NKJV

A really good parent is a provider, a counselor, an adviser, and when necessary, a disciplinarian.

—AUTHOR UNKNOWN

Psychiatrists tell us that discipline doesn't break a child's spirit half as often as the lack of it breaks a parent's heart.

—AUTHOR UNKNOWN

Single Moms

When Dad Can't Be There

The hand of our God is upon all those for good who seek Him.
—EZRA 8:22 NKJV

God's plan for parenting involves two people—a father and a mother. But there are times when dad can't be there because of death, divorce, business travel, an assignment in the military, or some other reason. In times like these, mothers who parent on their own shoulder the burden of fear, loneliness, and parenting problems. Yet these single moms tend to be more candid with their children, much more likely to admit their mistakes and seek forgiveness, too.

If you have to parent your kids alone, look to God first. Build your family around godly principles. Connect with a church to strengthen your faith. Keep your toddler's tantrums in perspective by joining or forming a single parent group in your church to meet other single moms. Learn together to handle issues that arise in single-parent homes. Your church can give your children positive male role models, too. God's Word talks about prince Joash whose father died while Joash was an infant. The high priest became the young boy's mentor. Because of that influence, "Joash did what was right in the sight of the LORD" (2 Chronicles 24:2 NKJV). The godly mentors in your church can have a positive affect on your kids, too.

Children in suddenly single parent homes can often experience feelings of insecurity and loss. So keep your children informed about family issues. For continuity, make as few changes in living arrangements and schedule as possible. Give your kids a sense of belonging by reminding them of family history, traditions, and events. If extended family lives elsewhere, informally adopt an elderly person from church as a grandparent.

A single mom must often work outside the home, too. Daycare facilities are one option for childcare. Choose the best one you can realistically afford. Visit different facilities on busy days to watch for staff-child interaction. Childcare by relatives may be another option. Set some basic guidelines; then let your relative use his or her judgment to handle anything else that arises. Holding down a job means there's less time for housework, too. Set priorities. Let others help with the chores. Keep the visible surfaces clean—let dust bunnies hide a bit longer. Simplify mealtime. Involve kids in the preparation and clean-up. Save the big, from-scratch meals for holidays and birthdays.

When dad can't be there, remember, "your Maker is your husband, the LORD of hosts is His name" (Isaiah 54:5 NKJV). With God's help you can tackle the job of single mothering and do it well, too.

I Will

Realize that though single parenting is more challenging, it can also be rewarding.

yes   _no_

Understand that single moms can form strong bonds with their kids in many ways.

yes   _no_

Acknowledge that even when parenting alone, I am never alone, for God is with me.

yes   _no_

Trust God to guide and strengthen me if I must parent my children alone.

yes   _no_

Look for the options God has given me to make single parenting easier.

yes   _no_

Remember that my children need godly male role models when dad isn't around.

yes   _no_

Things to Do

 Enroll your kids in art or play therapy to vent their emotions about dad's absence.

 Carry a cell phone that only your child can access. Keep that phone on to stay connected.

 To strengthen relationships, join your child for lunch at daycare or school on special days.

 Strengthen family ties by making a family tree with relatives' photos on your refrigerator.

 Take care of yourself. Hire a babysitter to give yourself some personal alone time.

 Show appreciation for those who have helped you during dad's absence: give flowers, notes, hugs.

Things to Remember

You will forget the shame you felt earlier; you will not remember the shame you felt when you lost your husband. The God who made you is like your husband.

ISAIAH 54:4–5 NCV

I will pay you back for those years of trouble . . . You will praise the name of the LORD your God, who has done miracles for you.

JOEL 2:25–26 NCV

The LORD watches over the strangers; He relieves the fatherless and widow; but the way of the wicked He turns upside down.

PSALM 146:9 NKJV

Leave your fatherless children, I will preserve them alive; and let your widows trust in Me.

JEREMIAH 49:11 NKJV

A father of the fatherless, a defender of widows, is God in His holy habitation.

PSALM 68:5 NKJV

Since we're creatures of Day, let's act like it. Walk out into the daylight sober, dressed up in faith, love, and the hope of salvation.

1 THESSALONIANS 5:8 THE MESSAGE

We can feel abandoned and orphaned, unheard from and insignificant in the great big world. But God whispers . . . and we know that we are safe, because none of us are ever without help.

—BRENDA WILBEE

As a mom who parents alone, you're in charge of your child's memories—of dad, of family, of goals accomplished. Endeavor to make those memories good ones.

—JUDY MITCHELL

Patience

Take Time

It is better to be patient than to be proud.

—ECCLESIASTES 7:8 NCV

Did you ever wonder why it takes nine months for a baby to grow to full term during pregnancy? There are many documentable, scientific reasons. It takes time for cells to multiply and divide, for bodily systems to develop and function properly. There are emotional and practical reasons for a long gestation period, too. It takes time for parents to get used to the idea of a new person joining the family. It takes time to get the how-to books purchased, the baby's room painted, and the hospital bag packed. But God probably had another reason for giving women nine months to become moms. He probably wanted moms to learn patience while it was still an easy thing to do.

Patience, according to the dictionary, is the art of "willingly suppressing annoyance when confronted with delay." Nine months is a long delay when it comes to waiting for something. Yet most pregnant women accept that wait without much complaint—at least until the last month or so. Almost anyone can wait patiently for something if you know *when* the something is supposed to happen.

It's harder to be patient when you're in a rush, late for an appointment, and your teen is dawdling in the bathroom, primping in front of the mirror for the umpteenth time, and you have no idea on the planet when he or she will emerge to finally announce, "I'm ready." For moms with toddlers, toe-tapping impatience creeps up on you in other ways. The incessant "Why?" and whine of wee ones can melt a mom's patience faster than a hot breeze on a soft-serve cone.

But God wants moms and kids to learn to be patient. Why? Because God is patient. Peter reminded first century Christians that "we are saved because our Lord is patient" (2 Peter 3:15 NCV). Paul informed his readers in Rome that God "patiently stayed with those people he was angry with" (Romans 9:22 NCV), those who had sinned and purposely turned against Him. Paul told Timothy of his personal experience with God's unlimited patience, too, noting "his patience with me made me an example for those who would believe in him" (1 Timothy 1:16 NCV). God knows how hard it is to be patient with those who willfully choose their own way, who put off time and again doing what has been asked of them. Yet God chooses to be patient, and because God wants you to be like Him, He wants you to be patient, too.

But patience isn't an easy lesson to learn. Because of our technological society, kids today often expect instant everything. Microwave meals make waiting for after-school snacks a thing of the past. Online surfing for research information makes waiting in a check-out line at the library unnecessary. Video games give instant fun; ATMs give instant cash; text notes fly back and forth with instant messaging. How can you teach kids patience when they're surrounded by instant everything? One way comes to mind—make them wait for some things. Refuse to be pushed into doing something just because other families are doing it. Set standards, and stick to them. Don't allow your kids to get their ears pierced or date at a younger age just because society says it's okay. Teach your kids that it's okay to wait for some things that are really important—their first car, a telephone in their room, a driver's license, a new skateboard, a pair of Nike's.

God's Word says that you can also find patience if you slow down and take a time out. When confronted with delay, when overwhelmed with whines, "rest in the LORD, and wait patiently for Him; do not fret . . . it only causes harm" (Psalm 37:7–8 NKJV). Draw upon your experience as a mom-in-waiting. Take a deep breath; count to ten; give yourself time to focus on God instead of on the delay or whatever is causing you to become impatient. Remember, patience is a choice.

So choose to be patient. Try not to be in such a hurry all the time. Choose to focus on God, and wait without fretting. You did it for nine months while awaiting your little ones. You can do it again, too. Take time to be patient.

I Will

Thank God for His patience with me.

      yes   no

Ask God to remind me to take a time out when I'm feeling impatient.

      yes   no

Be aware of those things that cause me to fuss, fret, and fume.

      yes   no

Remind myself that others have had to wait for me at times, too.

      yes   no

Remember that patience is a choice God wants me to make.

      yes   no

Focus on God and wait without fretting.

      yes   no

Things to Do

☐ *Write James 5:7–8 on a card. Post it as a patience reminder.*

☐ *Purchase small items as patience treats. Distribute the treats when your kids exhibit patience.*

☐ *Ask your kids to list items you should wait patiently for: stoplights, birthday presents, suppertime.*

☐ *Read 1 Samuel 13:5–14. Discuss the result of Saul's impatience.*

☐ *Make popcorn on the stovetop instead of in the microwave to help kids learn patience.*

☐ *Put some wet towels on a clothesline. While they dry, talk about waiting patiently.*

☐ *Put together a jigsaw puzzle. Take several days if necessary to avoid impatience and frustration.*

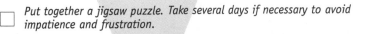

Things to Remember

God will strengthen you with his own great power so that you will not give up when troubles come, but you will be patient.

COLOSSIANS 1:11 NCV

Admonish the unruly, encourage the fainthearted, help the weak, be patient with everyone.

1 THESSALONIANS 5:14 NASB

Be joyful because you have hope. Be patient when trouble comes, and pray at all times.
Romans 12:12 NCV

The LORD will wait, that He may be gracious to you; and therefore He will be exalted, that He may have mercy on you . . . Blessed are all those who wait for Him.

ISAIAH 30:18 NKJV

Dear friends: Lead with your ears, follow up with your tongue, and let anger straggle along in the rear.

JAMES 1:19 THE MESSAGE

Wait on the LORD; be of good courage, and He shall strengthen your heart; wait, I say, on the LORD!

PSALM 27:14 NKJV

See how the farmer waits for the precious fruit of the earth, waiting patiently for it until it receives the early and latter rain. You also be patient.

JAMES 5:7–8 NKJV

Always be humble, gentle, and patient, accepting each other in love.

EPHESIANS 4:2 NCV

I wait for the LORD, my soul waits, and in His word I do hope. My soul waits for the Lord more than those who watch for the morning.

PSALM 130:5–6 NKJV

We are hoping for something we do not have yet, and we are waiting for it patiently.

ROMANS 8:25 NCV

The Spirit produces the fruit of love, joy, peace, patience, kindness, goodness, faithfulness, gentleness, self-control. There is no law that says these things are wrong.

GALATIANS 5:22–23 NCV

It is good that one should hope and wait quietly for the salvation of the LORD.

LAMENTATIONS 3:26 NKJV

Patience strengthens the spirit, sweetens the temper, stifles anger, extinguishes envy, subdues pride, bridles the tongue.

—GEORGE HORNE

How necessary it is that we wait on our God continually. Saul lost his kingdom for want of two or three hours' patience.

—MATTHEW HENRY

Happiness

The Elusive Dream

I will be happy because of you; God Most High.

—PSALM 9:2 NCV

The American Declaration of Independence states that we have a God-given right to the pursuit of happiness. Many people spend their lives pursuing this dream. Some folks look for happiness in possessions. Lotteries and gambling casinos flourish because some people believe having lots of money will ensure true happiness. Some people believe happiness can be found in pleasurable experiences. Others think happiness is synonymous with power and control.

Families are not exempt from this search for happiness either. Some moms try to find happiness by living vicariously through their own children. These kids and moms can end up in some difficult relationships because the boundaries between mother and child become blurred by codependencies. In addition, fad diets and quick-weight-loss schemes flourish because many women depend on physical beauty or size to feel happy. Yet happiness ultimately eludes them all.

Though moms may pursue happiness in many ways, God's Word says there's only one sure way to find it: "Whoever trusts the LORD will be happy" (Proverbs 16:20 NCV). Searching for happiness by yourself won't work, Mom, because it puts too much emphasis on *you* instead of on God. Searching for constant happiness is like wandering through life with your head down, looking only at your own feet. It's a selfish way to spend your life, and you'll miss a lot along the way, too.

God wants you to have worthier goals in life. Instead of seeking the surface dream of happiness, God's Word calls moms to a life of deep, abiding joy. The words of an old Sunday school song proclaim that by putting Jesus first in your life, then caring for Others, and looking out for Your own happiness last, you'll find true J O Y. By taking the focus off yourself and serving God and others first, you'll often find an unexpected result, too—happiness.

Try this. Instead of putting yourself first, give God first place. Rather than thinking about what your children can do for you, concentrate on what you can do for them. Introduce them to Jesus. Teach them God's Word. Let them see by your example how to serve others. Help them understand that true happiness is not found in the newest computer game or coolest skateboard. True happiness comes from knowing God, from trusting Him, and living for Him. As you teach your children God's lessons about joy and happiness, you'll be thinking less about yourself. Serving, giving, loving with your whole heart. Now that's guaranteed to make you happy.

I Will

Surrender my desire for happiness to God and trust Him. *yes* _____ *no* _____

Think less about myself and more about Him and others. *yes* _____ *no* _____

Ask God to forgive me for my self-centeredness. *yes* _____ *no* _____

Examine what it means to serve God with my whole heart. *yes* _____ *no* _____

Notice the needs of those around me. *yes* _____ *no* _____

Be patient and pray for my children's me-first attitudes. *yes* _____ *no* _____

Recognize the futility of the world's way for finding happiness. *yes* _____ *no* _____

Things to Do

☐ *Watch TV with your children. Discuss what you see about finding happiness.*

☐ *Tell a friend how you have found happiness in Jesus.*

☐ *As a family, give some of your possessions to a mission or shelter.*

☐ *Make a list of ways your family can serve others. Do some of these together.*

☐ *Work with your children to secretly help a neighbor.*

☐ *Read 1 Peter 4:7–11. Ask God to help you serve this way.*

☐ *Write a song about happiness. Use a familiar tune. Sing it with your children often.*

Things to Remember

Those who want to do right more than anything else are happy, because God will fully satisfy them.

MATTHEW 5:6 NCV

Happy are those who are like this; happy are the people whose God is the LORD.

PSALM 144:15 NCV

May the righteous be glad and rejoice before God; may they be happy and joyful.

PSALM 68:3 NIV

Happy are those who are helped by the God of Jacob. Their hope is in the LORD their God.

PSALM 146:5 NCV

The LORD has done great things for us, and we are very glad.

PSALM 126:3 NCV

You changed my sorrow into dancing. You took away my clothes of sadness, and clothed me in happiness.

PSALM 30:11 NCV

We are never so happy or so unhappy as we suppose.
—FRANCIS, DUC DE LA ROCHEFOUCAULD

Happiness is like a cat. If you try to coax it or call it, it will avoid you. But if you pay no attention to it . . . you'll find it rubbing against your legs.
—WILLIAM BENNETT

Talents and Abilities

Building Blocks

In Christ you have been made rich in every way, in all your speaking and in all your knowledge.

—1 CORINTHIANS 1:5 NCV

Plastic, interlocking blocks come in a variety of sizes, shapes, and colors to encourage children of all ages to build everything from simple towers to complex designs with moving parts. Kids play for hours with these blocks, pawing through piles of plastic pieces to find the exact one needed to complete a masterpiece.

Just as manufacturers provide variety in sets of interlocking building blocks, so God has provided variety in the talents and abilities He gives to His children. According to 1 Corinthians 12:1–11 all of God's children (including you) possess a special spiritual ability, uniquely given by God, to glorify Him and help others. These spiritual gifts include such things as an ability to teach, serve others, organize things, give with abandon, encourage, or show kindness. Romans 12 lists other spiritual gifts, too. God has given you at least one of these abilities. In order to put that talent to use, pray and ask Him to show you what your gift is and how you can best use it.

God also gives natural abilities in other areas. If you think about it, you can probably remember one or two things you attempted in the past that were soaring successes. Those successes are probably tied to a hidden talent, ability, or aptitude. You've probably had that talent your whole life. In fact, most young children, if allowed to choose, will prefer to do the things for which they already possess a natural ability. You've probably seen this in your kids. One child excels in sports while another grasps concepts with astonishing swiftness. Some kids sing well while others express themselves eloquently with an artist's brush. Children like these are already beginning to operate within their talents and abilities.

But some kids are late bloomers. They can't seem to find a niche where they excel. Some moms are late bloomers, too. The famous French chef Julia Child knew nothing about cooking until her late thirties. Grandma Moses, the renowned primitive artist, never lifted a brush until she was more than seventy years old. If you or your kids are unsure about what talents you each may have, don't despair. The music you hear, the stories you tell, the books you read, and the activities you take part in will broaden your imaginations and open your eyes to see where talents may lie. So don't hesitate. Whether you build a simple tower or a complex structure, use the talent blocks God has given you to make your life a masterpiece that glorifies Him.

I Will

Acknowledge that every child of God has a special gift from Him.

yes — *no* —

Ask God to show me the spiritual gifts He has given me.

yes — *no* —

Thank God for my obvious natural abilities.

yes — *no* —

Commit to using my gifts for His glory and to help others, too.

yes — *no* —

Be aware of other natural abilities or talents that may lie dormant in my life.

yes — *no* —

Encourage my children to find the gifts God has given them.

yes — *no* —

Relax and enjoy the talents God has given me.

yes — *no* —

Things to Do

☐ *List several things that you and your kids do well. Post this talent reminder prominently.*

☐ *Purchase Charles Stanley's Bible study guide* Ministering Through Spiritual Gifts *to determine your spiritual gifts.*

☐ *Play with your food. See which family member is the most artistic with mashed potatoes.*

☐ *Read Luke 19:11–27. Discuss why it's important to recognize and use your talents.*

☐ *Look at the pictures in a magazine and guess what each person's talent might be.*

☐ *Ask another mom what spiritual gifts or natural abilities they see in you.*

Things to Remember

God never changes his mind about the people he calls and the things he gives them.

ROMANS 11:29 NCV

Each has a particular gift from God, one having one kind and another a different kind.

1 CORINTHIANS 7:7 NRSV

I have filled him with the Spirit of God in wisdom, in understanding, in knowledge, and in all kinds of craftsmanship.

EXODUS 31:3 NASB

As each one has received a gift, minister it to one another, as good stewards of the manifold grace of God.

1 PETER 4:10 NKJV

Well done, good and faithful servant; you were faithful over a few things, I will make you ruler over many things. Enter into the joy of your lord.

MATTHEW 25:21 NKJV

Since we have gifts that differ according to the grace given to us, each of us is to exercise them accordingly.

ROMANS 12:6 NASB

A garden uncared for soon becomes smothered in weeds; a talent neglected withers and dies.
—ETHEL R. PAGE

The real tragedy of life is not in being limited to one talent, but in the failure to use the one talent.
—EDGAR W. WORK

Career Decisions

To Be or Not To Be

Whatever you do, do it heartily, as to the Lord and not to men.
—COLOSSIANS 3:23 NKJV

If William Shakespeare voiced a common concern of moms today he might say, "To work or not to work outside the home: that is the question." While most moms in the 1940s stayed home to care for the house, children, garden, laundry, mending, and meals, researchers say that more than half of all moms today work outside the home at least part time. Some do so because of financial constraints—single moms usually have to work to make ends meet. Other moms work to stay up to date in their field—some professions change so frequently, a year away from the job would require major retraining.

If you're considering working outside the home, you're facing a major decision. Though God's Word does not give clear-cut answers about whether moms should work outside the home or not, Proverbs 31 indicates that wise wives are often involved in some business enterprises. Pray and ask God to give you wisdom as you look at job possibilities. Talk to your spouse about family needs and lifestyle. Do some major soul searching. Just as children are different, moms are different, too. Recognize that you will be doing your child a disservice if you stay at home feeling angry or isolated because you've lost your career. However, if you feel guilty or sad every time you have to leave the little one you've yearned for so long, you may want to look for ways to stay at home with your child at least for the first few years.

Because no one can care for your child as well as you can, consider your child's needs as you make your job decisions. Remember children need outside influences and exposure to different people to become well-rounded individuals. Though these experiences can come from playgroups in the park, daycare programs and preschool classes offer similar influences, too.

Also note that many jobs today give moms flexibility in balancing family and career. You don't have to shut out work options just because you've had a baby. Job sharing, maintaining an office in the home, reducing time spent on business travel by telecommuting, or working flexible hours at the office are creative ways to blend career and family time. In addition, part-time work is a viable option for many moms. If you work in your field one day a week, you'll still be able to keep up with changes in your profession. Part-time work may pay better, too. Working only three or four days a week for four hours each day will net as much pay as a forty-hour week because of the extra costs involved in childcare, travel, and lunches.

Look closely at your family's finances and lifestyle, too. If you take an outside job, will you be working for the basics or the extras? Recognize that the luxuries your income provides one year can become the perceived needs of the future. You don't have to keep up with the Joneses. How important really are those extra vacations, cars, toys, or restaurant meals out? Your children need your attention more than extra toys or clothes, too. Will your job give you quality time with them? Balancing work and home responsibilities can consume so much energy you won't have much left to play with your kids or invest in your spouse. Distributing family chores can help, but it will mean if you're at work and your husband's at home, you'll have to let him do things the way he wants or the chores might not get done at all.

If you choose to be a full-time, stay-at-home mom, don't let others make you feel guilty, saying you're wasting your life, training, or happiness to embrace motherhood. Instead, think of the money you'll save on childcare, transportation, or meals out by staying at home. Recognize that you can always use volunteer time to achieve skills you might need for a paying job later on, too.

To be or not to be a working mom, a stay-at-home mom. It's a big decision. Some moms are happy working outside the home; some are happier as career moms. Some enjoy doing a bit of both. Yet, the best mother for your kids is a happy one. Choose your career—and your happiness—with them in mind.

I Will

Trust God to guide me in my decisions about work.	_yes_	_no_
Recognize that I don't have to feel guilty about my work choices.	_yes_	_no_
Reevaluate the reasons I do or do not work outside the home.	_yes_	_no_
Consider the financial impact on family life with and without my work outside the home.	_yes_	_no_
Examine my attitudes toward all work.	_yes_	_no_
Seek ways to balance all my work and family time.	_yes_	_no_

Things to Do

- [ ] *Do a topical Bible study on work and female Bible characters: Lydia, Dorcas, Ruth, Deborah.*

- [ ] *To determine a possible career, make a checklist of your strengths, weaknesses, and family needs.*

- [ ] *Seek out a mentoring mom for her prayers and advice about working outside the home.*

- [ ] *To help you in making career decisions, ask your kids how they feel about working moms.*

- [ ] *Make work fun. At home see who can work faster: you washing dishes or kids cleaning up toys.*

- [ ] *To illustrate the value of all jobs, work together on a family project: remodeling, landscaping, or such.*

Things to Remember

We must work the works of Him who sent Me as long as it is day; night is coming when no one can work.

JOHN 9:4 NASB

When you enter a town . . . stay in one place, eating and drinking what they provide you. Don't hesitate to accept hospitality, because those who work deserve their pay.

LUKE 10:7 NLT

Six days you shall work, but on the seventh day you shall rest; in plowing time and in harvest you shall rest.

Exodus 34:21 NKJV

When we were with you, we gave you this rule: "Anyone who refuses to work should not eat."

2 THESSALONIANS 3:10 NCV

God is not unjust to forget your work and labor of love which you have shown toward His name, in that you have ministered to the saints, and do minister.

HEBREWS 6:10 NKJV

Begin using your hands for honest work, and then give generously to others in need.

EPHESIANS 4:28 NLT

Take care of your own business, and do your own work as we have already told you. If you do, then people who are not believers will respect you.

1 Thessalonians 4:11–12 NCV

Whatever your hand finds to do, do it with your might; for there is no work or device or knowledge or wisdom in the grave where you are going.

Ecclesiastes 9:10 NKJV

Each one's work will become clear; for the Day will declare it, because it will be revealed by fire; and the fire will test each one's work.

1 Corinthians 3:13 NKJV

In the morning sow your seed, and in the evening do not withhold your hand; for you do not know which will prosper.

Ecclesiastes 11:6 NKJV

Let the beauty of the LORD our God be upon us, and establish the work of our hands for us, yes, establish the work of our hands.

Psalm 90:17 NKJV

She watches over the ways of her household, and does not eat the bread of idleness. Her children rise up and call her blessed; her husband also, and he praises her.

Proverbs 31:27–28 NKJV

God gives every bird its food, but he does not throw it into the nest.
—Josiah Gilbert Holland

Good for the body is the work of the body, good for the soul the work of the soul, and good for either the work of the other.

—Henry David Thoreau

Time Management

Ticks and Tocks

So teach us to number our days, that we may gain a heart of wisdom. —PSALM 90:12 NKJV

An eccentric gentleman once kept a living room full of clocks. Visitors were greeted on the hour by the deafening noise of chirping cuckoos, chiming grandfathers, and bonging mantel clocks. If a visitor stayed overnight, the gentleman would make a circuit of the living room to silence the ticks and tocks. "It gives me great pleasure," the gentleman would say, "to stop time whenever I can."

Unfortunately time slips by, even if you've stopped the clocks, so moms need to be creative time managers. Get a jump on your day by beginning each morning with God. Fifteen minutes spent in prayer and Bible study will give you the strength, hope, guidance, and creativity every mom needs. Then, set aside a few moments for yourself. You'll look better, feel better, and have a better attitude for dealing with your family if you get some regular exercise. If you don't think you have enough time to spend time with God *and* to exercise, too, combine the two. Take a walk with a headset tuned to God's Word. Ride a bike or swim laps as you pray about your family, your children, your hopes and dreams.

To bring balance to the remainder of your day, follow a schedule. It doesn't have to be rigidly marked out to the minute. Block out chunks of time, using the 7:00 a.m. to 10:00 a.m. hours to get people and pets fed, beds and lunches made, laundry and dishes washed, and the house straightened up a bit. Use another 4–5 hour allotment to finish household chores, run errands, and pay bills. Sectioning off your day lets you accomplish chores and incorporate naptimes for little ones, too.

In addition, teach your children to manage their time. Announce that you're setting a kitchen timer five minutes before suppertime or bedtime. Your kids will learn to better budget their own time as they realize how much they can (or cannot) accomplish in those few moments. To keep your whole family on schedule, try posting a family calendar. Assign a separate color of highlighter to each family member. Fill the calendar with everyone's schedule information. Make sure your daily schedule incorporates the calendar's information, too, so that you don't miss birthday parties, doctor's appointments, or make your teen late for work.

Turning off the clocks won't stop time, so try following God's time management suggestion instead: Make the most of every moment, every day. Managing your time God's way might just yield some *extra* time, too. And who couldn't use that?

I Will

Admit that I can always do a better job of
managing my time.

      yes _____   *no* _____

Commit to starting my days with a focus on God.

      yes _____   *no* _____

Realize that setting aside time for daily exercise
will make me a healthier, happier mom.

      yes _____   *no* _____

Bring balance to my days by following a to do list
or daily schedule.

      yes _____   *no* _____

Be aware of the time wasters in my life.

      yes _____   *no* _____

Recognize that I can find spare time if I manage
my hours more wisely.

      yes _____   *no* _____

Things to Do

☐ *Set goals for this week to help manage time. Mark them off when you finish them.*

☐ *Set a timer when cooking supper to help kids understand the passage of time.*

☐ *When planning your schedule, remember to add some fun time to each day.*

☐ *Print* SPEND TIME WITH GOD *on a picture of a clock. Post this reminder near your bed.*

☐ *Try cluster scheduling: one day for all your shopping, one day for all doctors' appointments, and so on.*

☐ *Teach young kids how to tell time; teach military (twenty-four-hour) time to older kids.*

Things to Remember

LORD, remind me how brief my time on earth will be. Remind me that my days are numbered, and that my life is fleeing away.

PSALM 39:4 NLT

We live in an important time. It is now time for you to wake up from your sleep, because our salvation is nearer now than when we first believed.

ROMANS 13:11 NCV

Do not boast about tomorrow, for you do not know what a day may bring forth.

PROVERBS 27:1 NKJV

Make the most of every opportunity for doing good in these evil days.

EPHESIANS 5:16 NLT

You do not know what will happen tomorrow. For what is your life? It is even a vapor that appears for a little time and then vanishes away.

JAMES 4:14 NKJV

Be wise in the way you act with people who are not believers, making the most of every opportunity.

COLOSSIANS 4:5 NCV

Most time is wasted, not in hours, but in minutes. A bucket with a small hole in the bottom gets just as empty as a bucket that is deliberately kicked over.

—PAUL J. MEYER

God . . . shows us by the wise economy of His providence, how circumspect we ought to be in the management of our time, for He never gives us two moments together.

—FRANÇOIS FÉNELON

Kindness

Shine

Show mercy to others, be kind, humble, gentle, and patient.
—COLOSSIANS 3:12 NCV

In the fable of the sun and the North Wind, the wind claimed to be more powerful than the sun. To prove its point, the wind said it could remove a traveler's coat faster than the sun could. The battle began. The wind blew cold and hard. But the traveler merely hugged his coat more tightly around himself. Then the sun took its turn, shining its beams on the cold, shivering man. The warm, gentle kindness of the sun's rays accomplished much more than the blasting force of the North Wind. In mere moments the traveler warmed up and removed his coat.

Ah, the power of warmth and kindness. Every mom knows that her children need lots of these affirmative virtues. Yet, because children are flawed human beings, just like moms, it isn't always easy to be kind. Children make mistakes; they do stupid things; they cause problems; they fall short of their mothers' expectations. Unfortunately, if a child accidentally does something wrong and a mom is tired, frustrated, or angry, it's all too easy to use force to correct them. But forceful physicality, harsh words, and strident tones that belittle children are as ineffective with your kids as the blustering tactics of the North Wind on the traveler.

God's Word says that He shows everlasting kindness toward His children. While wandering in the wilderness, the ancient Israelites repeatedly ignored God. They forgot time and again how God had come to their aid. Their forgetfulness caused them to do stupid things, to fall short of God's expectations. Yet God answered their repeated shortcomings with great kindness, providing ways of escape from enemies, raining down food from heaven, opening up fountains of water in the desert. It's this same kindness God shows to all people despite our faults and shortcomings as He offers to make us His children.

Accordingly, ask God to give you His kindness so you can respond to your children the same way He does—edifying, encouraging, helping. Look for ways to show God's kindness to your kids. Praise them in front of someone. Surprise them and do their chores without complaint. Offer encouraging words, a pat on the back, time spent doing what they want to do. Kindness should never be haphazard or random, but an oft-occurring happening between you and your children. As the sun shone its warmth on the traveler, shine the warmth of kindness on your kids. You'll find that same warmth will spread from your kids to others, too.

I Will

Be thankful for God's kindness to me and my children. _____ yes _____ no

Trust God to replace harshness with His kindness. _____ yes _____ no

Accept that my children are not perfect and make mistakes. _____ yes _____ no

Try to view my children and others through God's eyes. _____ yes _____ no

Seek opportunities to show kindness to my children and others. _____ yes _____ no

Acknowledge I have faults and weaknesses just like my children do. _____ yes _____ no

Things to Do

☐ Plan some ways for you and your children to show kindness to others.

☐ Pray with your children, thanking God for specific ways He has been kind to you.

☐ Invite a neighbor who lives alone to share a family meal.

☐ Using a concordance, see how many Bible verses you can find about being kind.

☐ Make a poster that says: Be kind to each other. Hang it as a kindness reminder.

☐ Read Mark 10:13–16 to see how Jesus showed kindness to children.

☐ Keep a list of ways people show kindness to you. Thank God for them.

Things to Remember

Be kind and loving to each other, and forgive each other just as God forgave you in Christ.

EPHESIANS 4:32 NCV

I will tell of the kindnesses of the LORD, the deeds for which he is to be praised.

ISAIAH 63:7 NIV

She opens her mouth with wisdom, and on her tongue is the law of kindness.

PROVERBS 31:26 NKJV

A servant of the Lord must not quarrel but must be kind to everyone, a good teacher, and patient.

2 TIMOTHY 2:24 NCV

Make sure that nobody pays back wrong for wrong, but always try to be kind to each other and to everyone else.

1 THESSALONIANS 5:15 NIV

As we have opportunity, let us do good to all, especially to those who are of the household of faith.

GALATIANS 6:10 NKJV

The nicest thing we can do for our heavenly Father, is to be kind to one of His children.

—SAINT TERESA OF AVILA

God is too wise to ever make a mistake and too loving to ever be unkind.

—DUANE PEDERSON

Peace

Have to Have It

He Himself is our peace. —EPHESIANS 2:14 NKJV

A mom with one child visited a mom with six kids, observing the chaos of doors slamming, phones ringing, voices calling, doorbells chiming, kids fighting, and a baby crying. The mom of one was overwhelmed with the noise, but the mom of six seemed unperturbed. The mom of one asked, "How can you seem so peaceful when everything around you is falling to pieces?" And the mom of six replied, "This? This *is* peace at our house. No one's hurt. No one's sick. God's in control. What else do you have to have to have peace?"

The mother of six had a comical way of expressing it, but indeed, with God in control, whether you mother one child or many, peace is possible. While some may think of peace as a worry-free, lifelong bubble bath, spiritual peace goes deeper than physical elements. Romans 5:1 says that peace is more than an absence of trouble—it is a reality that brings harmony to life. True peace embodies a sense of wholeness and well-being that God's Word says is only available through a right relationship with God. True spiritual peace is a fruit of God's Holy Spirit and a portion of the armor of God that all Christians should wear. Christians receive God's peace through holy living, and this peace protects them from worry and fear.

Unfortunately a family's peace can often fall to pieces, especially when focus becomes faulty and hearts turn away from God because of outside influences. The negative focus of nagging is a peace thief. You stress over a child's hairstyle, your spouse's late arrival home from work, or the to do list that keeps growing. As you hyper-focus on the insignificant, your voice becomes more strident and insistent. Peace in your home evaporates.

Discontent can pull peace into pieces, too. The couch that was fine last week, the dishes that still work but are cracked and worn, the car that's over three years old—these items don't hold a candle to the neighbor's new and improved everything. *Why does she get it all and I don't?* you grumble, and peace slips out the front door. Think about jealousy's effect on your kids, too. One child thinks another received a better Christmas present, undeserved attention, or more privileges. The whining starts; the fights escalate; and peace between siblings flies out the window.

Yet sometimes the biggest peace breaker for a mom is fear—problems, struggles, or heartaches that scare you deep down. Jesus' disciples personally experienced this peace breaker. Mark 4:35–41 says these former skilled fishermen were caught in a storm on the sea. They'd fished in storms before. But this one was different. This storm was a killer, and Jesus' disciples were sure they were doomed. They cried out in fear and woke Jesus, who had been sleeping like a baby through the howling wind and raging waves. All it took was His "Peace! Be still!" spoken to the terrifying storm to bring it to a standstill. The disciples realized that as long as Jesus was with them they had no reason to abandon the power of peace for the sinking ship of fear. Peace can exist in the middle of a problem. Peace can be found in the hurly-burly. But how can a mom get that peace and hold on to it?

God's Word says that to make peace a reality you need to "pursue the things which make for peace" (Romans 14:19 NKJV). Fear paralyzes you and weakens your faith, so pursue trust in God. Dishonesty reaps distress—pursue honesty. Fighting makes people angrier—pursue harmony. Hurt feelings harbor grudges—pursue forgiveness. Discontent, nagging, and jealousy keep you focused on the negatives, so put God first every time to ensure a peaceful heart. Teach your kids these truths, too. Help them look for ways to live peaceably with each other by putting the negative aside and focusing on God and His way.

Your peace doesn't have to fall to pieces if you keep your eyes on God. His peace is powerful and never-ending. He's in charge of your days. And like the mom of six said, if God's in control, what else do you have to have to have peace?

I Will

Consider that true peace is found in more than
outward appearances.

yes _____ _no_ _____

Be thankful that peace is a gift of God's Spirit
available to me anytime.

yes _____ _no_ _____

Understand that God's peace can protect my heart
from worry and fear.

yes _____ _no_ _____

Acknowledge that my kids' and my actions and
attitudes can drive peace from our home.

yes _____ _no_ _____

Remind myself to pursue the things that will bring
peace to my home.

yes _____ _no_ _____

Things to Do

☐ _Copy Jesus' words from Luke 24:36 onto a card. Remember God's peace
offered to you._

☐ _Give the kids a nap, ignore the phone and doorbell, and take a
peaceful bubble bath._

☐ _As you tuck your kids into bed at night, envision yourself tucked into
God's peace._

☐ _Light a candle after your kids are asleep. Watch the flame and be
at peace._

☐ _Call a family meeting and brainstorm ways to make peace a priority
in your home._

☐ _Take a walk in the woods and find the peace that comes with the
quiet._

☐ _Pray and ask God for peace. Hear Jesus say to you, "Peace. Be still."_

Things to Remember

Acquaint yourself with Him, and be at peace; thereby good will come to you.

JOB 22:21 NKJV

Let the peace of God rule in your hearts, to which also you were called in one body; and be thankful.

COLOSSIANS 3:15 NKJV

The peace of God, which transcends all understanding, will guard your hearts and your minds in Christ Jesus.
Philippians 4:7 NIV

The LORD will give strength to His people; the LORD will bless His people with peace.

PSALM 29:11 NKJV

When people live so that they please the LORD, even their enemies will make peace with them.

PROVERBS 16:7 NCV

Those who love your teachings will find true peace, and nothing will defeat them.

PSALM 119:165 NCV

You will keep him in perfect peace,
whose mind is stayed on You, because
he trusts in You.

ISAIAH 26:3 NKJV

The meek shall inherit the earth, and
shall delight themselves in the
abundance of peace.

PSALM 37:11 NKJV

The LORD bless you and keep you; the
LORD make His face shine upon you,
and be gracious to you; the LORD lift up
His countenance upon you, and give
you peace.

NUMBERS 6:24–26 NKJV

"I will give peace, real peace, to those far
and near, and I will heal them," says the
LORD.

ISAIAH 57:19 NCV

Do your part to live in peace with
everyone, as much as possible.

ROMANS 12:18 NLT

The fruit of righteousness is sown in
peace by those who make peace.

JAMES 3:18 NKJV

Peace is full
confidence that
God is Who He says
He is and that He
will keep every
promise in His
Word.

—DOROTHY HARRISON
PENTECOST

Many people are
trying to make
peace, but that has
already been done.
God has not left it
for us to do; all we
have to do is to
enter into it.

—DWIGHT. L. MOODY

Feelings and Emotions

Peek-a-Boo

The mind set on the flesh is death, but the mind set on the Spirit is life and peace. —ROMANS 8:6 NASB

Babies like to play peek-a-boo. When they close their eyes, moms disappear; when they open their eyes, moms return—just like magic. Unfortunately moms and kids can't play peek-a-boo with feelings and emotions. You can't just close your eyes and make those pesky feelings disappear. Managing emotions takes a lifetime of experience.

Begin by considering how God made you and your kids. Everyone has feelings and emotions, but different personalities express those feelings in different ways. Some kids are extroverts—the ones in your family who make others smile. Other kids may explode in angry tantrums. Still others may be congenial pleasers who do what you ask, but bury their feelings in their busyness. All children, regardless of personality type, need reassurance that feeling their feelings is normal. They'll never be able to stop feeling certain emotions like love or anger, yet they need to learn that there are good and bad ways to express those feelings. God's Word gives examples from Jesus' life that illustrate appropriate ways to express emotions, like Jesus' joy in the presence of children, His sorrow over death, His anger at injustice, and His compassion for others.

Kids feel emotions at all ages, too. Infants sense your feelings. If you're happy, they're usually happy. But if you're nervous or fussy—watch out. Little ones will begin to fuss, too. Soothe both of your fussy feelings with a nap or change of scenery. Whispering in an ear sometimes works, too. If you find yourself constantly saying no to a toddler, the emotion of frustration may be running high. Shift gears and call in reinforcements: a babysitter or spouse to watch the kids while you take a walk. Let children know, too, that their inappropriate expressions of emotions cloud communication: If they whine, you won't listen; if they use foul language, you won't stay in the same room with them.

To find peaceful, godly feelings, concentrate on the good stuff. Arouse empathy in your kids as you talk about and pray for those who have experienced tragedy. Feelings of compassion can grow in your kids' lives when you actively look to ease someone's burden. Feelings of love and acceptance get a boost when hugs, smiles, and words of encouragement flow freely in your home. Encourage your kids to play peek-a-boo with little ones, too, because there's an emotion hidden in such play, too—the feeling of joy.

I Will

Rely on God to help me help my kids manage their emotions.

<u>*yes*</u>   <u>*no*</u>

Look for my kids' different personalities and ways of expressing their emotions.

<u>*yes*</u>   <u>*no*</u>

Be aware that my children need reassurance that feeling their feelings is normal.

<u>*yes*</u>   <u>*no*</u>

Be thankful for Jesus' example that teaches my children and me appropriate expressions of emotion.

<u>*yes*</u>   <u>*no*</u>

Realize that my kids are sensitive to my emotions and feelings.

<u>*yes*</u>   <u>*no*</u>

Learn to encourage my kids to feel good feelings.

<u>*yes*</u>   <u>*no*</u>

Things to Do

☐ *Ask your kids how they would feel if they lived somewhere without food or housing.*

☐ *Whenever you're afraid, record your feelings in a journal. Note your feelings after fear passes.*

☐ *Reduce emotional outbursts from toddlers by scheduling your errands to non-nap times.*

☐ *Surprise your child with happy playtime in the park—before they begin to whine for it.*

☐ *Make an emotions poster. Find stickers, magazine photos, and newspaper headlines that illustrate different feelings.*

☐ *Read Psalm 102:1–11 together. Talk about the feelings the Psalmist shared with God.*

Things to Remember

Search me, O God, and know my heart; try me and know my anxious thoughts; and see if there be any hurtful way in me.

PSALM 139:23–24 NASB

Lord, all my desire is before You; and my sighing is not hidden from You . . . Make haste to help me, O Lord, my salvation!

PSALM 38:9, 22 NKJV

How long shall I take counsel in my soul, having sorrow in my heart daily? . . . I have trusted in Your mercy; my heart shall rejoice in Your salvation.

PSALM 13:2, 5 NKJV

I pour out my complaint before Him; I declare before Him my trouble. When my spirit was overwhelmed within me, then You knew my path.

PSALM 142:2–3 NKJV

Why are you cast down, O my soul? And why are you disquieted within me? Hope in God; for I shall yet praise Him, the help of my countenance.

PSALM 43:5 NKJV

Be transformed by the renewing of your mind, that you may prove what is that good and acceptable and perfect will of God.

ROMANS 12:2 NKJV

The great thing to remember is that, though our feelings come and go, God's love for us does not.

—C. S. LEWIS

Explosions of temper, emotional cyclones, and needless fear and panic over disease or misfortune that seldom materialize, are simply bad habits.

—ELIE METCHNIKOFF

Loneliness

Kidnapped

God places lonely people in families. —Psalm 68:6 GOD'S WORD

The nightly news in a major city carried a story about a lonely mother who faked a kidnapping. Her children were grown and living elsewhere; her husband worked long hours at his job. The woman felt cut off, lonely, and depressed. She decided to commit suicide, but wanted proof beforehand that no one really cared. The woman called her husband's office claiming she had been kidnapped and telling him he had to pay a ransom for her release. To the woman's amazement her husband *did* care about her, raised the ransom money, *and* called the police. When officers stormed the address given for the ransom drop, they found the woman, uncovered the truth, and jailed her in a solitary confinement cell for faking a crime. The poor woman ended up lonelier than before.

Loneliness is a major problem for all moms. Mothering puts you in daily contact with kids but often keeps you out of daily touch with others. Though moms today meet more people in a year than their great-grandmothers met in a lifetime, the sense of isolation is growing. You've probably felt it yourself—that lonely-in-acrowd feeling. Your kids can feel lonely, too, especially if they're in transition between neighborhoods, schools, or activities.

To help you and your kids scale the walls of loneliness, remind yourselves that God has said, "I will never leave you nor forsake you" (Hebrews 13:5 NKJV). Turn to Him in prayer together, accepting His promised presence. Then *do* something. Call another mom and suggest a picnic with the kids. Reach out of your comfort zone to a visitor at church. Work toward building bridges of friendship, love, and caring. There may be others around you who are lonely, too, who would embrace a friendship if one were offered. Ask God to lead you and your kids to such people. Be sensitive to other leadings, too—those inner nudges to go visit someone, call somebody, or pop a note in the mail to someone else. The personal contact you extend and receive will help fill the hole of loneliness in your heart.

If you can't escape an attack of loneliness, set a timer for fifteen minutes. Whine, whimper, fuss, and moan to God about your loneliness for that quarter hour. But when the bell rings, *quit*. Take a shower. Go to the park with the kids. Bake some cookies. Make a phone call. Don't let you or your kids be kidnapped by loneliness. You're never alone; God is always there.

I Will

Recognize that loneliness is a major problem for all moms, not just me.

yes _____   no _____

Remind myself that God is always with me.

yes _____   no _____

Refuse to be kidnapped by loneliness.

yes _____   no _____

Help my kids fill their lonely hearts with reminders of God's love.

yes _____   no _____

Trust that an attack of loneliness will pass in time.

yes _____   no _____

Choose to have a positive attitude and do something about my loneliness.

yes _____   no _____

Show kindness and friendship to others who might be lonely, too.

yes _____   no _____

Things to Do

☐ *Organize a neighborhood block party. Have fun, build community spirit, and banish loneliness.*

☐ *Take your kids to visit someone in a convalescent home and ease someone else's loneliness.*

☐ *Fill a scrapbook with pictures of family, friends, neighbors. Refer to it to chase loneliness away.*

☐ *Sign up for an adult education course to make new friends and ease loneliness.*

☐ *Make a poster that says I'M NEVER ALONE. GOD IS ALWAYS WITH ME. Post this reminder prominently.*

☐ *To ease loneliness, invite two moms and their kids over to play and share together.*

Things to Remember

The LORD God said, "It is not good that man should be alone; I will make him a helper comparable to him."

GENESIS 2:18 NKJV

There's not a soul who cares what happens! I'm up against it, with no exit—bereft, left alone. I cry out, GOD, call out: "You're my last chance!"

PSALM 142:4–5 THE MESSAGE

God's presence is with people, and he will live with them, and they will be his people. God himself will be with them and will be their God.

REVELATION 21:3 NCV

The LORD your God, He is the One who goes with you. He will not leave you nor forsake you.

DEUTERONOMY 31:6 NKJV

Teach them to obey everything that I have taught you, and I will be with you always, even until the end of this age.

MATTHEW 28:20 NCV

I will not leave you all alone like orphans; I will come back to you.

JOHN 14:18 NCV

Loneliness is the first thing which God's eye named as not good.

—JOHN MILTON

The central purpose of Christ's life . . . is to destroy the life of loneliness and to establish here on earth the life of love.

—THOMAS WOLFE

Fear

All Shapes and Sizes

The LORD is my helper; I will not fear. What can man do to me?
—HEBREWS 13:6 NKJV

Sam cowered behind his mother's back. Just moments before he had loudly protested being called little, reminding everyone that he was in preschool, that he was "a big boy now." Yet at a quirky restaurant, the sight of a waitress tossing hot, oven-fresh rolls to customers reduced this brave schoolboy to a frightened four-year-old. Though older folks found the waitress's antics amusing, Sam's fear of being clobbered by hot, baked rolls sent him scurrying for cover.

Fear comes in all shapes and sizes, but as Sam's experience illustrates, not all people share all fears. Not all fears are bad, either, yet some fears need to be conquered. Fear can protect us from harm and danger, but it can also keep us from taking needed action. For example, the fear of falling may keep an older adult away from an ice skating rink, saving them from serious injury, yet the same fear of falling could keep a toddler from trying to take a few steps. To help your child through the fears of growing up, moms need to remember a few pointers.

Start by evaluating and conquering your own fears. Some moms are afraid of heights; some balk at the noise of power tools. Other moms are afraid of being home alone. One mother was involved in six car accidents in eighteen months. Afraid to drive again, this mom became a virtual prisoner in her suburban home. A six-week driver re-education class finally freed this mom from her fear. Another mother knew she was afraid of thunderstorms. She didn't want to pass this fear to her children, so, whenever a thunderstorm came, she would cuddle with her children in the living room, opening doors and windows to watch the lightening and hear the crack of the thunder. To keep from fearfully crying out, this mom would count the seconds aloud between the lightening flash and thunderclap, keeping up a constant discussion of what was happening throughout the storm. As a result, her presence with her children kept them from becoming frightened. She herself became less fearful of thunderstorms, too.

In any situation, face all your fears with prayer. Ask God to defeat the fears that set your knees knocking. Recall how God has faithfully helped you conquer other fears. Thank Him in advance for helping you overcome the fears you now face.

Consider the fearful situations that trouble your children, too. Treat all fears seriously, and never shame children for their fears. Instead, do whatever you can to alleviate them. If the dark scares your child, leave a nightlight on. If your child insists there's a monster in the closet, it could be because of a movie about monsters you recently rented from the video store. Remind yourself not to expose your child to scary movies until they are a bit older, and then open the closet door. Prove it's vacant. Give your child a big hug. Reassure them of your love, of God's constant presence with them. Sam's mother tucked him under her arm during the roll-throwing incident. Because of his mother's concern, by meal's end Sam was no longer fearful of flying rolls.

Be careful, too, about the language you use when talking to children about new situations. Some small children are terrified of going to sleep or of taking a rest because a pet has been put to sleep or an older relative was laid to rest. Be straightforward instead in discussions of death, telling children that their pet or relative is no longer living. If you have warned your children about the dangers of sharp objects that could cut them, talking about going for a hair*cut* could be a fearful situation, too. Say instead that your kids need to go make their hair look neat or pretty.

As your child grows up, new fears will replace old ones. Pay attention to your child's friends, to the games they play, to the television shows or movies they watch. Toys, movies, and TV shows come with age guidelines to help you protect your child from unnecessary fears. Even if a friend has access to these things, what may be acceptable for them may not be appropriate for your child. Fearful experiences affect each child differently. Stay alert to better help your children conquer their fears.

I Will

Remember that fear comes in all shapes and sizes.   yes _____ no _____

Understand that what makes someone else afraid may not frighten me.   yes _____ no _____

Acknowledge that fear can sometimes keep me from taking action when I need to.   yes _____ no _____

Consider that some fear is good to keep me and my family out of danger.   yes _____ no _____

Prayerfully evaluate the things that make me afraid.   yes _____ no _____

Ask God to show me ways to conquer my own fears.   yes _____ no _____

Things to Do

☐ *Role play these scary situations—a lost child, mommy gets hurt, a car accident.*

☐ *Tell your child one of your childhood fears and how you overcame it.*

☐ *Pray before every bedtime, asking God to give good dreams and good sleep.*

☐ *Ask your child to draw a picture of whatever is making him or her afraid.*

☐ *If someone's afraid of the dark, go outside at night. Look for fireflies or stars.*

☐ *Place a motion-sensor nightlight in a hallway or bathroom to chase away the darkness.*

☐ *Take a bathroom break after a nightmare to clear away the scary thoughts.*

Things to Remember

My peace I give to you; not as the world gives do I give to you.
Let not your heart be troubled, neither let it be afraid.

JOHN 14:27 NKJV

Fear not, for I am with you; be not dismayed, for I am your God.
I will strengthen you, yes, I will help you, I will uphold you.

ISAIAH 41:10 NKJV

*When I am afraid, I will trust you. I praise God
for his word. I trust God, so I am not afraid.
What can human beings do to me?*
Psalm 56:3–4 NCV

Do not fear, little flock, for it is your Father's good pleasure to
give you the kingdom.

LUKE 12:32 NKJV

Be strong and brave, and do the work. Don't be afraid or
discouraged, because the LORD God, my God, is with you.

1 CHRONICLES 28:20 NCV

With the Lord on my side I do not fear. What can mortals
do to me?

PSALM 118:6 NRSV

If an army surrounds me, I will not be afraid. If war breaks out, I will trust the LORD.

PSALM 27:3 NCV

My flesh and my heart may fail, but God is the strength of my heart and my portion forever.

PSALM 73:26 NASB

We stand fearless at the cliff-edge of doom, courageous in seastorm and earthquake, before the rush and roar of oceans, the tremors that shift mountains.

PSALM 46:2–3 THE MESSAGE

You will not fear any danger by night or an arrow during the day. You will not be afraid of diseases that come in the dark or sickness that strikes at noon.

PSALM 91:5–6 NCV

Do not be afraid. Stand still, and see the salvation of the LORD, which He will accomplish for you today.

EXODUS 14:13 NKJV

God has not given us a spirit of fear, but of power and of love and of a sound mind.

2 TIMOTHY 1:7 NKJV

When fear knocks at the door of the heart, send faith to open it, and you will find that there is no one there.

—AUTHOR UNKNOWN

So-called positive thinking is no weapon against fear. Only positive faith can rout the black menace of fear and give life a radiance.

—MARION HILLIARD

Priorities

What's Most Important

First seek the counsel of the LORD.   —1 KINGS 22:5 NIV

So much to do; so little time. Is that how you feel as a busy mother? If it's too hard to find some quiet time at home with or without your kids, it may be time for you to prioritize.

Basic priorities are necessary to keep our families running smoothly. To prioritize well look at your life, your activities, your schedule, and your family's needs. Decide what's vitally important, what can be left for another time, and what is truly unnecessary. Life never stands still while you're working through your priorities. Other things will come along that have to be added to your sort list, forcing you to change some priorities and stretch others until you can feel like an acrobat. So begin well. Make sure your priority list places God at the top. Time spent with Him should be your first priority. Then let God and His Word be the yardstick you use to set your other priorities. Choose to put on the priority list only those things that will honor and glorify Him.

Then make some personal choices before trying to prioritize your children and their schedules. If you work outside the home, decide which is most important to you, your job or your home life. How much time and effort will you choose to spend on each? If you are a stay-at-home mom, how much time can you spend just on your children? If you have fifteen minutes to spare, which is more important to you, cleaning the oven or playing a game with your child? Realize that other moms may make different choices based on their own personalities, lifestyles, or economic situations. Their choices may not work for you and vice versa.

Look closely at your children's priorities. They may be skewed heavily toward activities that place unrealistic demands on the family. Their priorities may be pulling them off to church functions, school programs, or civic clubs. While all of these activities are commendable, you may need to restrict your child's involvement in some activities if family life gets too hectic. Trees need pruning in order to grow strong and healthy; so, too, priorities may necessitate some pruning of activities to strengthen family relationships. By helping your children prioritize their school time, free time, and home time, you'll find they'll be more successful in those few, well-chosen activities than if they tried to do everything available to them. Unburden yourself and your children. Prioritize your lives to find what's most important.

I Will

Ask God to show me what is most important
to Him.   *yes*   *no*
                                                      _____   _____

Evaluate my family's activities.   *yes*   *no*
                                                      _____   _____

Acknowledge the need to spend more time reading
God's Word with my children.   *yes*   *no*
                                                      _____   _____

Trust God to be involved with all my family's
activities.   *yes*   *no*
                                                      _____   _____

Begin every day praying for wisdom in setting
priorities.   *yes*   *no*
                                                      _____   _____

Realize that my children won't like giving up some
activities.   *yes*   *no*
                                                      _____   _____

Things to Do

☐ *Plan a special meal to discuss setting family priorities.*

☐ *Work with your children to prioritize their activities, deleting unimportant things.*

☐ *Read Luke 10:38–42. What can this passage teach you about setting priorities?*

☐ *Post a family calendar in the kitchen. Write down all activities, places, and times.*

☐ *Talk with your children about their activities. How is God working through them?*

☐ *Pray that God will work in all your activities for His honor and glory.*

Things to Remember

Be very careful how you live. Do not live like those who are not wise, but live wisely.

EPHESIANS 5:15 NCV

Be sure that you live in a way that brings honor to the Good News of Christ.

PHILIPPIANS 1:27 NCV

Set your mind on things above, not on things on the earth. For you died, and your life is hidden with Christ in God.

COLOSSIANS 3:2–3 NKJV

Do not turn to the right or the left; Remove your foot from evil.

PROVERBS 4:27 NKJV

The thing you should want most is God's kingdom and doing what God wants. Then all these other things you need will be given to you.

MATTHEW 6:33 NCV

Jesus answered, "Love the Lord your God with all your heart, all your soul, and all your mind. This is the first and most important command."

MATTHEW 22:37–38 NCV

Well arranged time is the surest mark of a well arranged mind.
—ISAAC PITMAN

Where no plan is laid, where the disposal of time is surrendered merely to the chance of incident, chaos will soon reign.
—VICTOR HUGO

Kids and Money

Cash and Caring

You cannot serve both God and worldly riches.

—Matthew 6:24 NCV

Learning to name the colors, to identify animals sounds correctly, and to count from one to ten are skills most moms teach their toddlers. But did you know toddlers can also learn lessons about cash and caring through charity?

Because your children will eventually have money of their own, helping set up financial guidelines while they're still young is a good idea. To teach children how to manage their money and share their material blessings with others, experts suggest giving weekly allowances. A five-year-old can start with fifty cents a week. Add an additional fifty cents each year at birthdays. Having a set amount and a set time for raises limits teasing for more money throughout the year. When your child reaches double-digit birthdays, make the increases a dollar per year. Some families continue allowances into college years; others stop such stipends once a child begins a part-time job.

Other families do not give weekly allowances, but pay their children for extra work. Children are not paid for doing regular chores—that would be like paying yourself to mow your own lawn. Rather, these children earn extra money for doing chores that the family might have to hire out anyway. In this type of financial arrangement children learn the basics of a boss-employee relationship and learn basic negotiation skills when determining what each job will pay.

Teach your child to be a good money manager and one who shares with others by encouraging your child to take a tithe off the top of any money he or she receives, whether gifts, allowance, or wage earnings. Let your child know that this is God's money, money to be given to your church or other charitable organization or ministry. Beginning this biblical practice early in life will make it easier for your children to continue tithing when they get older. Help your children prioritize their money for other things, too. Suggest they set aside 10 percent for charity, 50 percent for college savings, 20 percent for a special item (bicycle, car, stereo, guitar), and 20 percent for personal use (outings, gifts).

God's Word contains many lessons on money, too. Moses reminded the Israelites that God "gives you power to get wealth" (Deuteronomy 8:18 KJV). Jesus said, "It is more blessed to give than to receive" (Acts 20:35 NKJV). The book of Proverbs is filled with admonitions to philanthropy, reminding readers "generous people will be blessed" (Proverbs 22:9 NCV). So help your children learn the lessons of cash and caring. The blessings will be worth it.

I Will

Thank God for all the blessings He has given me.   _yes_   _no_

Remind myself that God is concerned with how I use
my money.   _yes_   _no_

Consider that I can teach my children valuable
lessons about generosity and money management.   _yes_   _no_

Acknowledge that God wants me to be blessed in
my finances.   _yes_   _no_

Know that God, as the Creator, is the one who owns
everything.   _yes_   _no_

Comprehend that I can only have one master:
God or money.   _yes_   _no_

Things to Do

☐ *Read Luke 21:1–4 together. Discuss what you learn from the widow and
her pennies.*

☐ *Make a mission's box for everyone's loose change. After a month, give
it all away.*

☐ *Let children decide what ministry should receive their tithe. Investigate
several options, including your church.*

☐ *Play games involving paper money—Life, Monopoly, Pay Day—and let
your child be banker.*

☐ *Talk about what you can and cannot buy with a million dollars.*

☐ *Let older children keep track of the family finances on a $10
outing day.*

Things to Remember

Whoever loves money will never have enough money; whoever loves wealth will not be satisfied with it.

ECCLESIASTES 5:10 NCV

Those who desire to be rich fall into temptation and a snare . . . The love of money is a root of all kinds of evil.

1 TIMOTHY 6:9–10 NKJV

Give me neither poverty nor riches . . . lest I be full and deny You, and say, "Who is the LORD?" Or lest I be poor and steal.

PROVERBS 30:8–9 NKJV

Don't wear yourself out trying to get rich . . . Wealth can vanish in the wink of an eye. It can seem to grow wings and fly away like an eagle.

PROVERBS 23:4–5 NCV

Use your worldly resources to benefit others and make friends. In this way, your generosity stores up a reward for you in heaven.

LUKE 16:9 NLT

Good people will be generous to others and will be blessed for all they do.

ISAIAH 32:8 NLT

The saying is that he who gives to the poor, lends to the Lord. But it may be said, not improperly, the Lord lends to us to give to the poor.

—WILLIAM PENN

All our money has a moral stamp . . . The uses we put it to, the spirit in which we spend it, give it a character which is plainly perceptible to the eye of God.

—THOMAS STARR KING

Wisdom

Hot Burners and Sharp Lids

Behold, the fear of the Lord, that is wisdom, and to depart from evil is understanding. —JOB 28:28 NKJV

All wise parents want to share their wisdom with their kids. While teenagers may resist stories that teach obvious lessons, most small children listen intently to the nuggets of wisdom you convey. After all, you are the stove maven who warns of the dangers of hot burners. You are the bathtub wizard who knows that soap stings when it gets in your eyes. You are the sharp object expert who advocates caution around knives, scissors, broken glass, and aluminum can lids. You, Mom, are wisdom personified for these insights.

But those wise things aren't really wisdom things, are they? They're just everyday knowledge, right? Not really. Many of the things you accept as common knowledge or factual information are actually things you've learned and experienced over the years. When you remember how you got your burned fingers and stinging eyes and try not to injure yourself again in the same way, you are exhibiting *wisdom*—the coupling of good judgment with information, facts, truths, or principles.

Think about some of the older moms you respect or want to be like. They care for their kids and homes with seemingly little effort. If you feel like you're stumbling along in the dark, do something wise. Go to the older moms you respect, and ask them to share their secrets with you. The areas in your life that cause you confusion right now might possibly be areas in which these older moms are more discerning. Their years of experience can teach you what things might sting when your kids are school age, which burners will be hot when jealousy or unfairness surfaces, or how to handle the sharp can lids of two teenagers co-existing under one roof.

Proverbs 4:11–12 also encourages every mom to teach her children wisely and lead them along paths that won't cause confusion, distraction, or stumbling. But to lead a child in wisdom, a mom first has to find wisdom herself. Asking an older mom for advice is a good start, but don't forget to ask the One who is the source of all wisdom, too. Whenever you pray and ask God for wisdom and insight, picture yourself as a little child, standing beside your all-wise Father, listening for His voice to guide and direct you. He'll give you His wisdom, so go ahead, and ask for God's common knowledge. He'll gladly keep you away from those hot burners and sharp can lids. After all, that's what wise parents do.

I Will

Be thankful for all of my life experiences, for they can teach me wisdom. ___yes___ ___no___

Try to blend knowledge and good judgment to find wisdom in my days. ___yes___ ___no___

Expect God to give me the wisdom I seek. ___yes___ ___no___

View myself as someone growing in wisdom and insight. ___yes___ ___no___

Seek and learn from the insight and wisdom of older moms. ___yes___ ___no___

Recognize that I might have wisdom to share with other younger moms, too. ___yes___ ___no___

Things to Do

☐ *Read one chapter from Proverbs with your kids. Memorize one of the wise sayings.*

☐ *List three areas in your life as a mom where you'd like more wisdom.*

☐ *Meet with a friend or mentor to discuss ways to improve your mothering insights.*

☐ *Join a mom's Bible study group to learn God's wisdom and new mothering skills.*

☐ *Copy James 1:5 onto a card and keep it where you can see it often.*

☐ *With your kids, look in Proverbs for verses about wisdom. Discuss wisdom's benefits together.*

Things to Remember

From a wise mind comes wise speech;
the words of the wise are persuasive.

PROVERBS 16:23 NLT

The mouths of the righteous utter
wisdom, and their tongues speak justice.
The law of their God is in their hearts;
their steps do not slip.

PSALM 37:30–31 NRSV

The tongue of the wise uses knowledge
rightly, but the mouth of fools pours
forth foolishness.

PROVERBS 15:2 NKJV

If any of you needs wisdom, you should
ask God for it. He is generous and
enjoys giving to all people, so he will
give you wisdom.

JAMES 1:5 NCV

I am guiding you in the way of wisdom,
and I am leading you on the right path.
Nothing will hold you back; you will
not be overwhelmed.

PROVERBS 4:11–12 NCV

The wisdom that is from above is first
pure, then peaceable, gentle, willing to
yield, full of mercy and good fruits,
without partiality and without
hypocrisy.

JAMES 3:17 NKJV

To know is not to
be wise. Many men
know a great deal,
and are all the
greater fools for it
. . . But to know
how to use
knowledge is to
have wisdom.

—CHARLES H. SPURGEON

The road to
wisdom? Well, it's
plain and simple to
express: Err and err
and err again; But
less and less and
less.

—PIET HEIN

Problems

Backhanded Blessings

You therefore must endure hardship as a good soldier of Jesus Christ.   —2 Timothy 2:3 NKJV

The bills are overdue. The baby has been sick for more than a week. Work either wears you out or is nonexistent. The kids seem to bicker all the time. The car is in the shop. You've had fights with your spouse and haven't even had a moment to yourself to get your hair done. After experiencing weeks like this, would you believe such problems could be blessings in disguise? God's Word says they can be—if you learn a lesson from King Asa.

King Asa had been a strong man of faith, following God and seeking His guidance while still a young, inexperienced king, trusting God for power and strength to overcome his enemies. Then, when Asa was fifteen years into his reign, when life was good and Asa's spiritual life was at an all-time high, God came to him and promised him peace, prosperity, and rest from war. What mom wouldn't want blessings like that?

So King Asa and his people lived in peace. For twenty years there were no wars. For twenty years trade increased, the economy grew, the private sector flourished. The people had a few pennies left over every month to fritter away on non-essentials. King Asa grew rich, too. As he surveyed his kingdom, Asa had no perceived needs at all.

But, in the thirty-sixth year of his reign, King Asa ran into trouble. A neighboring king put up barriers to keep people from entering or leaving Asa's country. Trade was interrupted. War was imminent. King Asa called for help. Problem is, Asa called on the wrong guy. After twenty years of blessing and peace, King Asa no longer had the habit of calling on God for daily help, guidance, power, and strength. For twenty years Asa hadn't had to ask anyone for anything. Now, when faced with a problem, God was no longer the first person Asa ran to. Instead, King Asa sent a message to the king of Aram offering to pay him to fight off the advances of the neighboring king. Though the king of Aram drove off Asa's enemy, God was not pleased with Asa's choice. He sent a messenger to the king saying, "Asa, you did a foolish thing, so from now on you will have wars" (2 Chronicles 16:9 NCV).

God was true to His word. From that point on King Asa's country was overrun with wars. But Asa again stubbornly refused to call on God for help. So life got a little harder. In the thirty-ninth year of his rule, King Asa developed "a disease in his feet. Though his disease was very bad, he did not ask for help from the LORD" (2 Chronicles 16:12 NCV). God's Word says King Asa died two years later. This king, who had started out faithfully following God during the tough times of his reign, fell away from his faith when life was easy; King Asa died a broken, sick, careworn old man.

Consider this: Would you take God's blessings for granted, like Asa did, if they were always there in abundance? If things always ran smoothly for you, would you be forgetful of God's provision? Asa had peace on every side; you may have days of healthy kids and smooth sailing, too. Yet Asa's peaceful years brought about a misplaced self-reliance that was his undoing when problems finally surfaced. Problems and troubles can remind you of your limitations and of God's powerful, abundant help, guidance, grace, favor, strength, and wisdom awaiting you each time you pray. The bills, bickering, and broken-down car might be the very things that keep you on track spiritually, reminding you only God can pull everything back together when your world is falling apart.

When things are stirred up in your family, neighborhood, church, school, work, or personal life, hold on to the promise that King Asa forgot: "The Lord searches all the earth for people who have given themselves completely to him. He wants to make them strong" (2 Chronicles 16:9 NCV). Turn your troubled heart to God. Ask Him for His strength to deal with sick kids and stressful situations. Thank Him for His blessings in good times, but also for the backhanded blessings of trouble, too. Those problems might just be God's blessings in disguise.

I Will

Remind myself that everyone has problems
sometime in life.

yes _no_

Consider that problems and troubles might be
blessings in disguise.

yes _no_

Acknowledge that too much of a good thing might
result in taking it for granted.

yes _no_

Remember that only God can give me the help I
need to face my problems.

yes _no_

Recognize the danger of forgetting about God
when things are going well.

yes _no_

Things to Do

☐ *Read 2 Chronicles 14–16 with your kids. Discuss King Asa's faith in troubled times.*

☐ *List ways that your family's problems could have beneficial effects now and later.*

☐ *Borrow a hymnbook. Look up the songs about trials and troubles. Learn one together.*

☐ *Seek out another mom who shares similar struggles. Pray together about your problems.*

☐ *Memorize one of God's promises about problems: John 16:33, Psalm 22:24, or Job 23:10.*

☐ *Draw pictures of blessings you take for granted. Thank God for these things.*

Things to Remember

In this world you will have trouble, but be brave! I have defeated the world.

JOHN 16:33 NCV

Though I walk in the midst of trouble, You will revive me; You will stretch out Your hand against the wrath of my enemies, and Your right hand will save me.

PSALM 138:7 NKJV

He does not ignore those in trouble.
He doesn't hide from them but
listens when they call out to him.
Psalm 22:24 NCV

God gave you the honor not only of believing in Christ but also of suffering for him, both of which bring glory to Christ.

PHILIPPIANS 1:29 NCV

Just as the sufferings of Christ are ours in abundance, so also our comfort is abundant through Christ.

2 CORINTHIANS 1:5 NASB

I consider that the sufferings of this present time are not worthy to be compared with the glory which shall be revealed in us.

ROMANS 8:18 NKJV

When you have many kinds of troubles, you should be full of joy, because you know that these troubles test your faith, and this will give you patience.

JAMES 1:2–3 NCV

Our fight is not against people on earth but against the rulers and authorities and the powers of this world's darkness, against the spiritual powers of evil in the heavenly world.

EPHESIANS 6:12 NCV

We also have joy with our troubles, because we know that these troubles produce patience. And patience produces character, and character produces hope.

ROMANS 5:3–4 NCV

I take pleasure in infirmities, in reproaches, in needs, in persecutions, in distresses, for Christ's sake. For when I am weak, then I am strong.

2 CORINTHIANS 12:10 NKJV

God blesses the people who patiently endure testing. Afterward they will receive the crown of life that God has promised to those who love him.

JAMES 1:12 NLT

In the day of prosperity we have many refuges to resort to; in the day of adversity, only One.

—HORATIUS BONAR

God is sufficient for all our needs, for every problem, and for every difficulty, for every broken heart, and for every human sorrow.

—PETER MARSHALL

Witness

Go and Tell

You are My witnesses. Is there a God besides Me?

—ISAIAH 44:8 NKJV

The most effective witnesses for God are those whose lives have been changed. God's Word tells about a man who was so tormented by evil spirits he could no longer live with his family, but made his home in the cemetery. When Jesus came to his town, the man ran to meet Him, and Jesus healed him. The man begged to travel with Jesus, but was told instead, "Go home to your friends, and tell them what great things the Lord has done" (Mark 5:19 KJV). The man obeyed. People heard the man's story and were so amazed at the changes in his life they, too, began to follow Jesus.

If you have experienced God's touch in your life in any way, big or small, God wants you to be a witness for Him, too. God can use your changed life to draw people, especially your family, to Him. You may not fully understand what happened to you when God touched you, when you accepted His gift of salvation, or when you felt God's reassurance in a frightening situation. But you can share your personal experiences, your witness. You don't need to badger someone into making a decision about God before they're ready, either. When those who know you see the difference God has made in your life, they'll be amazed like the folks in Mark 5. In fact, they may be so interested they'll ask to know more.

As a mom one of your callings is sharing God and His gifts with your kids. Since children often understand actions better than words, they need to see the impact that God's presence makes in your heart and life as well as hear about God and His gift of salvation. Lead your kids gently to God by letting His love shine through your actions. Talk to your kids about God's great love and Jesus' death that paid for their sins and guarantees eternal life. Let them know that the changes they see in your life come because God has given you His love.

You can give your witness away in other ways, too. Start a Bible study in your neighborhood. Share a Christian book with a friend. Find a church that welcomes children and makes God real to them. Use daily teachable moments to respond to your children's questions with information about God. God has changed your life in many ways. Now's your chance to share that news with someone else. Go ahead; stay home—and tell.

I Will

Examine my relationship with Jesus, making sure
that I have accepted God's gift of salvation.   _yes_   _no_

Believe that God can use me to bring others to Him.   _yes_   _no_

Understand that sharing my witness with others
includes sharing it at home, too.   _yes_   _no_

Ask God daily to let me be a witness to someone
in some way.   _yes_   _no_

Thank God for those who have shared their
witness with me.   _yes_   _no_

Show by my life that God has changed me.   _yes_   _no_

Things to Do

☐ *Study 1 Corinthians 15:3–4 to discover the gospel message in a nutshell.*

☐ *Write out a testimony of what God has done for your kids and you.*

☐ *Talk with another Christian about some ways to share your faith.*

☐ *Enroll kids in a church class so they'll grow with God and in faith each week.*

☐ *Set aside some God time. Read God's Word, pray, answer kids' questions about God.*

☐ *Invite neighbors to your home at Easter time. Read aloud the story of the resurrection.*

☐ *Light a candle to remind your family to be God's light in a dark world.*

Things to Remember

You will receive power and will tell people about me everywhere—in Jerusalem, throughout Judea, in Samaria, and to the ends of the earth.

ACTS 1:8 NLT

Day after day, in the temple courts and from house to house, they never stopped teaching and proclaiming the good news that Jesus is the Christ.

ACTS 5:42 NIV

My lips shall utter praise, for You teach me Your statutes. My tongue shall speak of Your word, for all your commandments are righteousness.

PSALM 119:171–172 NKJV

Go home to your family and tell them how much the Lord has done for you and how he has had mercy on you.

MARK 5:19 NCV

We are Christ's ambassadors, and God is using us to speak to you. We urge you, as though Christ himself were here pleading with you, "Be reconciled to God!"

2 CORINTHIANS 5:20 NLT

Always be ready to answer everyone who asks you to explain about the hope you have, but answer in a gentle way and with respect.

1 PETER 3:15–16 NCV

Common humanity should prevent none of us from concealing the great discovery which grace has enabled us to make.

—CHARLES HADDON SPURGEON

O use me, Lord, use even me, just as Thou wilt, and when, and where.

—FRANCES R. HAVERGAL

Safety

Dorothy's Wisdom

He shall give His angels charge over you, to keep you in all your ways. —PSALM 91:11 NKJV

As a tornado approaches in *The Wizard of Oz,* Dorothy's grandmother wrings her hands in desperation. Dorothy is nowhere to be found; danger is imminent. Moms can relate to the grandmother's longing to protect her granddaughter, because it is a God-given, instinctive desire. You're the nurturer, the primary caregiver for your children, just as God is your primary caregiver. He keeps you safe by keeping an eye on you, just like you keep your children safe by your watchful care, too.

That watchful care includes routines you may take for granted. Routine helps provide safety and security in different ways. For small children, saying together "Hands up, doors closed, belts on, let's go!" is a routine that gets everyone safely into the car. Routines inside your home can build emotional security, too. Using the same seats at meals or doing the same chores every day may be boring to you. Yet these routines, along with everyday love and acceptance, will give your children a sense of security that will help carry them through the tough teen years.

But don't forget the physical aspects of safety, too. Ensure your child's physical safety at home by crawling through the house on your hands and knees, looking for dangerous objects or situations. Keep poisons and cleaning supplies in high, locked cabinets. Block stairs off from crawling toddlers. Children are more likely to taste things if they're hungry, so keep substances like prescription medicines out of reach, too. Throw out all broken toys so loose parts don't become a choking hazard. Toddlers want to feed themselves, so give them tidbits that are the size of the tip of your pinkie finger. Even if your kids don't chew those bites well, those tiny bites can be swallowed whole.

Despite all your best efforts, accidents will happen. Keep emergency information posted by the telephone. Include the family's first and last name, address, phone number, burglar alarm code, and doctor's telephone number. Teach your children how to connect with emergency services by dialing 911. Remember to stay calm in an emergency, too. Don't panic. Take deep breaths. The way you handle an emergency will affect your children. If you act scared, your child may panic, too.

Even if the carpet's worn and the paint needs refreshing, with a few preventive measures your home can be a haven of safety. And, as Dorothy ultimately declared in the *The Wizard of Oz*, "There's no place like home." Especially a safe one.

I Will

Understand that a sense of safety is one of the basic needs of all people.

yes _____ _no_ _____

Appreciate that God looks out for me, cares for me, and provides for me.

yes _____ _no_ _____

Remember how safe I felt recalling my childhood traditions and routines.

yes _____ _no_ _____

Trust God to help me childproof my home to make it a safe place.

yes _____ _no_ _____

Understand that acceptance and love are as necessary for emotional security as daily routines.

yes _____ _no_ _____

Remember that accidents and emergencies will happen, even in a childproof home.

yes _____ _no_ _____

Things to Do

☐ _Check to make sure my child's walk/ride to school is as safe as possible._

☐ _Prepare a card with emergency information to place beside each telephone._

☐ _Role-play with my children how to report a fire, a break-in, or other emergency._

☐ _Purchase a small fire extinguisher for kitchen use and keep it fully charged._

☐ _Teach my children a car safety routine: Hands up, doors closed, belts on, let's go!_

☐ _Pray without ceasing in every dangerous situation._

Things to Remember

The King of Israel, the LORD, is with you; you will never again be afraid of being harmed.

ZEPHANIAH 3:15 NCV

Even though I walk through the valley of the shadow of death, I will fear no evil, for you are with me; your rod and your staff, they comfort me.

PSALM 23:4 NIV

God is our protection and our strength. He always helps in times of trouble.

PSALM 46:1 NCV

You have been my protection, like a strong tower against my enemies. Let me live in your Holy Tent forever. Let me find safety in the shelter of your wings.

PSALM 61:3–4 NCV

During danger he will keep me safe in his shelter. He will hide me in his Holy Tent, or he will keep me safe on a high mountain.

PSALM 27:5 NCV

I will both lie down in peace, and sleep; for You alone, O LORD, make me dwell in safety.

PSALM 4:8 NKJV

How protected are God's children when they are in the center of His directive will! How safe are those whose lives are hid with Christ in God!

—WALTER B. KNIGHT

If the Lord be with us, we have no cause of fear. His eye is upon us, His arm over us, His ear open to our prayer—His grace sufficient, His promise unchangeable.

—JOHN NEWTON

Love

A Comfort Cover

Love one another as if your lives depended on it.

—1 PETER 1:22 THE MESSAGE

Do you have a favorite blanket? A soft, scrunchie, warm, cuddly coverlet that you crawl under when you're sure you're dying of a cold? Your kids may have such a blanket—handmade in soft baby colors, hugged and washed and dried until it's almost worn through in places. Cuddly blankets bring comfort, security, warmth, and softness to a cold, scary world. And so does love.

Love is grounded in God's nature. When your heart aches, there's a wonderful comfort found in connecting with God, wrapping His love and tenderness around you like a blanket. But God's love doesn't stop there. Through His words and actions, God shows people how to love others just like He loves them. To learn to love this way takes a lifetime of following God's example. As a mom, you are God's living example of love to your children. Your kids look to you for the same comfort, connection, and tenderness you find with God, to learn how to love Him more, and to learn how to love others, too. It's a big job; but God has promised to help you do it.

When your kids are small, start loving lavishly. Despite old wives' tales, too much love has never spoiled an infant. During a child's first year, whenever your baby cries, respond to him or her in love as quickly as possible. A year of milk and kisses, diapers and toys, constant reassurance and happy smiles, will assure your child of your love.

As children get older, they'll equate love with the provision of daily needs—*Since my mom loves me she will feed me, house me, and keep me safe.* But growing children have needs for love's reassurance in other areas, too. When a child is old enough to understand a reprimand, they are also old enough to make an apology and receive forgiveness in order to restore a loving relationship. To help your child learn to love, you'll have to admit your faults, too, and ask forgiveness when you've said or done something to hurt them. You willingness to admit your weaknesses will increase your children's love for you.

Your love and acceptance are more important to your child than anything. Because of that love, your child will respond like you do, too. If your child sees you spending time with God in prayer and Bible study and loving Him above all things, your child will be more apt to have a personal, loving relationship with God. Let love blanket your family with God's tenderness.

I Will

Acknowledge that all love comes from God. _yes_ _no_

Appreciate that God's love extends to all people including my family and me. _yes_ _no_

Recognize that learning to love is a lifetime experience. _yes_ _no_

Understand that my kids can learn to love others through my example. _yes_ _no_

Consider that love involves ongoing forgiveness and growth. _yes_ _no_

Accept that giving and receiving love is necessary to building trust in a relationship. _yes_ _no_

Things to Do

☐ *With your kids take turns finishing the statement "I love you more than . . ."*

☐ *Make up nicknames for your kids that pinpoint a positive: Smiley, Blue Eyes, Curly.*

☐ *Write an I-love-you note. Hide it in a child's backpack or coat pocket.*

☐ *Learn to say "I love you" in four different languages. Use the phrases often.*

☐ *Call a local radio station and dedicate a song to your kids—with love.*

☐ *Devise an I-love-you signal: beep the horn three times, touch your nose, cross your arms.*

☐ *Surprise your kids by doing a chore they dislike as your special love gift.*

Things to Remember

This is My commandment, that you love one another as I have loved you.

JOHN 15:12 NKJV

Love is patient and kind. Love is not jealous, it does not brag, and it is not proud. Love is not rude, is not selfish, and does not get upset with others.

1 CORINTHIANS 13:4–5 NCV

Love each other like brothers and sisters. Give each other more honor than you want for yourselves.

ROMANS 12:10 NCV

All of you should be in agreement, understanding each other, loving each other as family, being kind and humble.

1 PETER 3:8 NCV

The most important piece of clothing you must wear is love. Love is what binds us all together in perfect harmony.

COLOSSIANS 3:14 NLT

Let us love one another, for love is of God; and everyone who loves is born of God and knows God. He who does not love does not know God.

1 JOHN 4:7–8 NKJV

Love is hundreds of tiny threads which sew people together through the years.

—SIMONE G. SIGNORET

Love is the one business in which it pays to be an absolute spendthrift: Give it away, throw it away; splash it over; empty your pockets; shake the basket; tomorrow you'll have more than ever.

—AUTHOR UNKNOWN

Perseverance

A New Chapter

May the Lord direct your hearts into the love of God and into the steadfastness of Christ. —2 THESSALONIANS 3:5 NASB

For many children, unraveling the mystery of reading is exciting. As they become more proficient in reading skills, kids discover stories about boys and girls and dogs named Spot. But the ultimate excitement in reading comes when a child can finally read a chapter book just like the big kids. Following a story through chapter after chapter is an exciting adventure.

Mothering is an exciting adventure, too. As you persevere through motherhood's ups and downs, you realize that a two-month-old won't stay two months old forever; toddlers or teens won't be toddlers or teens forever, either. Your children move from one experience to another, and you come along for the ride, moving from one chapter to another of mothering.

While it's perfectly natural for moms to feel overwhelmed and stretched thin at times during this lifelong journey, never forget that you're not alone. God has promised to be with you always. Remember, too, that your kids are God's kids first. He gave them to you for this time so that you could love them, nurture them, and introduce them to Him. You're in this parenting thing for the long haul, too, so pray hard, play lots, and love always. No matter whether your kids are tots or teens, give them your best.

Different stages of mothering will require different skills, schedules, and focused attention, too. Pray for daily guidance to handle the constant changes. Limit the number of your outside activities while your children are young, to give you more time with them. Give ever-expanding responsibilities to your growing kids, even if they make messes or mistakes, otherwise you'll still be cutting your children's meat at dinnertime when they're teenagers. Use your children's behavior patterns to your advantage, too. All kids behave better the closer you get to gift-giving holidays. Use these times for encouragement. Reward good behavior with copious praise. Scribble happy faces in lipstick on bathroom mirrors. Pop loving reminders into lunch boxes. Whether they're four or fourteen, invest your time in your kids now, while they still have their greatest need for you.

Most of all remember a mom's perseverance through all the stages of mothering will have life-changing effects on your kids. You've seen football players wave at television cameras and mouth, "Hi, Mom." That's persevering power—moving through the chapters of mothering with hugs and laughter, tears and prayers, love and kindness, guidance and determination. Mothering is an exciting adventure that requires your commitment and perseverance. What will the next chapter hold for you?

I Will

Appreciate the wonderful gift God has given me
in my children.

yes _____ no _____

Take advantage of every day, for my children will
never be this age again.

yes _____ no _____

Remind myself that I'm never alone when mothering
my children—God is always with me.

yes _____ no _____

Ponder the amazing opportunities I have mothering
my children through so many stages of life.

yes _____ no _____

Consider the importance of giving my children my
best at all times.

yes _____ no _____

Concede that as my children's needs change, I
need to make mothering adjustments, too.

yes _____ no _____

Things to Do

☐ Take a photo of you and your kids as a reminder of this stage of life together.

☐ Write a prayer asking God to help you glorify Him and persevere in mothering your kids.

☐ Read aloud a chapter book. See how the main character's life changes in each chapter.

☐ Swap stories about persevering through mothering with an older mom or grandmom.

☐ Watch a video like Rudy or Radio with your kids, and discuss what perseverance means.

☐ Celebrate your children. Serve party foods. Play games. Make a memory that lasts a lifetime.

Things to Remember

Let us throw off everything that hinders and the sin that so easily entangles, and let us run with perseverance the race marked out for us.

HEBREWS 12:1 NIV

Believe in the LORD your God, and you shall be established; believe His prophets, and you shall prosper.

2 CHRONICLES 20:20 NKJV

Be careful to obey the rules and laws the LORD gave Moses for Israel. If you obey them, you will have success. Be strong and brave. Don't be afraid.

1 CHRONICLES 22:13 NCV

He will give eternal life to those who persist in doing what is good, seeking after the glory and honor and immortality that God offers.

ROMANS 2:7 NLT

Pursue a righteous life—a life of wonder, faith, love, steadiness, courtesy. Run hard and fast in the faith. Seize the eternal life, the life you were called to.

1 TIMOTHY 6:11–12 THE MESSAGE

We pray that you will also have great wisdom and understanding in spiritual things so that you will live the kind of life that honors and pleases the Lord.

COLOSSIANS 1:9–10 NCV

Even the woodpecker owes his success to the fact that he uses his head and keeps pecking away.

—COLEMAN COX

The difference between perseverance and obstinacy is, that one often comes from a strong will, and the other from a strong won't.

—HENRY WARD BEECHER

Books in the Checklist for Life series

Checklist for Life
ISBN 0-7852-6455-8

Checklist for Life for Graduates
ISBN 0-7852-6186-9

Checklist for Life for Leaders
ISBN 0-7852-6001-3

Checklist for Life for Teachers
ISBN 0-7852-6002-1

Checklist for Life for Teens
ISBN 0-7852-6461-2

Checklist for Life for Women
ISBN 0-7852-6462-0

Checklist for Life for Men
ISBN 0-7852-6463-9